THE
MANDALA
ASTROLOGICAL
TAROT

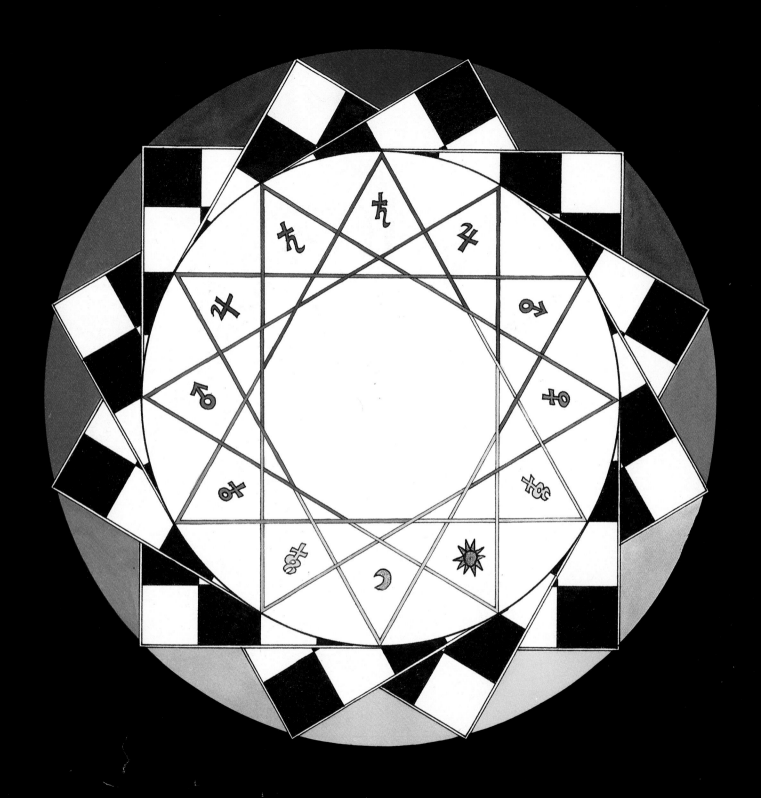

THE
MANDALA
ASTROLOGICAL
TAROT

A.T. MANN

Thorsons
An Imprint of HarperCollins*Publishers*

Thorsons
An Imprint of HarperCollins*Publishers*
77–85 Fulham Palace Road,
Hammersmith, London w6 8jb

First published by Macmillan London Limited 1987
This edition published by Thorsons 1997
1 3 5 7 9 10 8 6 4 2

© Elm Grove Books Limited 1987
Text © A. T. Mann 1987
Illustrations © A. T. Mann 1987

A. T. Mann asserts the moral right to
be identified as the author of this work

A catalogue record for this book
is available from the British Library

ISBN 0 06 2505831

Manufactured in China

The Mandala Astrological Tarot Cards

THE MAJOR ARCANA

FOOL	19, 34, **37**, 128, 141, 147
MAGICIAN	34, **39**, 141, 147
HIGH PRIESTESS	34, **41**, 128, 147
EMPRESS	34, **43**, 128, 147, 153
EMPEROR	34, **45**, 128, 139, 147
HIGH PRIEST	34, **47**, 128, 147
LOVERS	34, **49**, 128, 147, 153
CHARIOT	34, **51**, 128, 153
STRENGTH	34, **53**, 128
HERMIT	34, **55**, 128, 153
WHEEL OF FORTUNE	17, 34, **57**, 153
JUSTICE	34, **59**, 128, 141
HANGED MAN	34, **61**
DEATH	17, 34, **63**, 128
TEMPERANCE	34, **65**, 128
DEVIL	34, **67**, 128
TOWER	34, **69**, 128, 137, 139, 147
STARS	34, **71**, 128
MOON	17, 34, **73**, 128, 147
SUN	34, **75**, 153
JUDGEMENT	34, **77**, 147
WORLD	34, **79**, 128

THE COURT CARDS

WAND QUEEN	27, 80, **85**
WAND KING	27, 80, **85**
WAND PRINCE	27, 80, **85**
WAND PRINCESS	80, **85**, 153
PENTACLE QUEEN	27, 80, **87**
PENTACLE KING	27, 80, **87**
PENTACLE PRINCE	27, 80, **87**
PENTACLE PRINCESS	80, **87**
SWORD QUEEN	27, 80, **89**
SWORD KING	27, 80, **89**
SWORD PRINCE	27, 80, **89**
SWORD PRINCESS	80, **89**
CUP QUEEN	27, 80, **91**, 153
CUP KING	27, 80, **91**
CUP PRINCE	27, 80, **91**, 153
CUP PRINCESS	80, **91**, 153

THE MINOR ARCANA

WAND ACE	92, **97**, 153
WAND TWO	92, **99**, 153
WAND THREE	92, **99**
WAND FOUR	92, **99**
WAND FIVE	92, **101**, 153
WAND SIX	92, **101**
WAND SEVEN	92, **101**
WAND EIGHT	92, **103**
WAND NINE	92, **103**
WAND TEN	92, **103**
PENTACLE ACE	92, **105**
PENTACLE TWO	92, **107**
PENTACLE THREE	92, **107**
PENTACLE FOUR	92, **107**
PENTACLE FIVE	92, **109**
PENTACLE SIX	92, **109**
PENTACLE SEVEN	92, **109**, 153
PENTACLE EIGHT	92, **111**
PENTACLE NINE	92, **111**
PENTACLE TEN	92, **111**
SWORD ACE	95, **113**
SWORD TWO	95, **115**, 153
SWORD THREE	95, **115**, 153
SWORD FOUR	95, **115**
SWORD FIVE	95, **117**
SWORD SIX	95, **117**
SWORD SEVEN	95, **117**
SWORD EIGHT	95, **119**, 153
SWORD NINE	29, 95, **119**
SWORD TEN	95, **119**
CUP ACE	95, **121**
CUP TWO	95, **123**
CUP THREE	95, **123**
CUP FOUR	95, **123**
CUP FIVE	95, **125**
CUP SIX	95, **125**
CUP SEVEN	95, **125**
CUP EIGHT	95, **127**
CUP NINE	95, **127**
CUP TEN	95, **127**, 153

Contents

INTRODUCTION
TO
TAROT

Tarot is an ancient system of divination using cards. Divination means *from the divine* on the assumption that prophecy is a sacred process throughout the universe. People in all early cultures attempted to foresee the future because their lives depended upon it. They used anything available to determine their fate, including tea leaves, bones, stones, the flights of birds, making marks in the earth, observing clouds in the sky, the entrails of animals, sand, dice of various descriptions, and the stalks of plants.

Although the origin of tarot cards has been attributed to the ancient Chaldeans or Egyptians, the earliest known decks date back to fourteenth century Europe, and are the forerunners of modern playing cards. It is certain that in India and the Far East religious images were illustrated on cards which were tied together with cord, and that such cards were brought back to Europe by the Knights Templars after the Crusades. This was about the time when block printing became used, therefore it is obvious that printed decks did not exist before then. Early decks were one-off and unique to the artist, produced in the same way as books were copied by scribes.

The first tarot decks had between 50 and 80 cards, the most typical having 78 cards. This standard set contained 40 numbered cards from ace to 10, 16 court cards depicting Kings, Queens, Knights and Pages or Princesses, all divided into four suits like our modern playing cards. In addition there were 22 picture cards called trumps, deriving from the Italian *trionfi*, the circular triumphal procession in Roman times, or alternately from the *triumphator* or high priest who presided over such celebrations. Twenty-one of the trumps

are numbered and one, called Le Mat or the Fool, is unnumbered.

The trumps are also called the major arcana or greater mysteries, while the numbered cards from ace to 10 are called the minor arcana or lesser mysteries. Although tarot cards were also used for playing games the fact that they contained hidden meanings has been central to their continuing popularity – they span the range of human endeavour from play to the mysteries of the universe. The tarot trumps are:

O	Fool	XI	Justice
I	Magician	XII	Hanged Man
II	High Priestess	XIII	Death
III	Empress	XIV	Temperance
IV	Emperor	XV	Devil
V	High Priest	XVI	Tower
VI	Lovers	XVII	Stars
VII	Chariot	XVIII	Moon
VIII	Fortitude	XIX	Sun
IX	Hermit	XX	Judgement
X	Wheel of Fortune	XXI	World

The images in early tarot decks reflect the structure of the medieval world with kings, queens, chariots, lovers, high priestesses, popes, magicians and fools. The four suits were depicted as common instruments used by everyone, such as cups, swords, wands and coins. Thus the tarot deck provided a cast of characters together with a complement of ritual implements, possessing both an obvious and harmless meaning for the simple and a more complex magical interpretation for initiates.

There is, however, a more powerful and potent reason for the duality of tarot symbolism. When tarot cards were first introduced into Europe, the Church was fanatically opposed to any alternative belief systems, all of which were considered heretical. Those found holding different beliefs or reading banned books were often tortured and killed for their trouble. It was not until the end of the sixteenth century that mathematics was allowed as a subject of higher learning at universities – it was previously considered a magical art. The fact that for simple people tarot was a harmless game did not initially protect it; there was widespread banning of the cards throughout Europe in the fifteenth century.

For initiates, of course, tarot was a way for transmitting hidden knowledge of ancient mystery cults which were also conveyed by the Masons and Rosicrucians. The Church tried to eradicate surviving traces of pagan nature cults in Europe, and certain tarot images such as the high priestess and the empress incorporated images from earth mother cults from earlier times. As we now know, most women persecuted as witches in the Middle Ages were simply practitioners of herbalism, earth mother cults and natural agricultural magic. Fortunately, the rapid spread of Renaissance humanism in following centuries encouraged a tolerance of the ideas and symbols of the past as well as an interest and acceptance, albeit grudgingly, of alternative religious images and concepts from the East.

An overwhelming majority of the people in the Middle Ages were illiterate, and religious ideas were transmitted through images, in paintings, carvings and stained glass windows in the churches. There was an obvious parallel and similarity in form between religious and heretical symbolic art.

A very powerful medieval concept was that of the millennium. The process of the creation of the world as described in the Bible naturally led to the conclusion that at the end of the world there would be a Last Judgement in which the worthy would ascend to heaven while evildoers would be enchained in hell. The duality of heaven and hell was influential in bringing the people into line with Church doctrine and was reinforced in cathedral imagery, such as terrifying gargoyles carved in stone. One early tarot deck which differed greatly from the traditional but shows this medieval idea is the Baldini-Mantegna deck, which although attributed to the famous artist Mantegna, was not drawn by him. The deck is composed of five classes of 10 cards, each class describing a hierarchy of governing qualities. The classes are as follows:

Class A: The Celestial System

xxxxx The First Cause, xxxxviiii The First Movement, xxxxviii The Sphere of the Fixed Stars (the zodiac), xxxxvii Saturn, xxxxvi Jupiter, xxxxv Mars, xxxxiiii The Sun, xxxxiii Venus, xxxxii Mercury, xxxxi The Moon.

Class B: The Virtues

xxxx Faith, xxxxviiii Hope, xxxviii Charity, xxxvii Justice, xxxvi For-

titude, xxxv Prudence, xxxiiii Temperance, xxxiii Cosmology, xxxii Chronology, xxxi Astronomy.

Class C: The Sciences
xxx Theology, xxviiii Astrology, xxviii Philosophy, xxvii Poetry, xxvi Music, xxv Arithmetic, xxiiii Geometry, xxiii Rhetoric, xxii Logic, xxi Grammar.

Class D: The Muses
xx Apollo, xviiii Clio, xviii Euterpe, xvii Melopomene, xvi Thalia, xv Polyhymnia, xiiii Erato, xiii Terpsichore, xii Urania, xi Calliope.

Class E: The Conditions of Life
x The Pope, viiii Emperor, viii King, vii Doge, vi Knight, v Gentleman, iiii Merchant, iii Goldsmith, ii Valet, i Beggar.

The sequence of 50 cards describes the structure of the universe from the First Cause to man. It is clear from the Baldini-Mantegna deck that even if it is at variance with the traditional tarot structure, it has many similar cards, and was clearly used as an educational or instructional device as well as for divination.

Also in the Middle Ages the Gypsies (a corruption of Egyptians) introduced exotic eastern symbols and concepts to tarot from their Indo-European homelands. Gypsies carried and disseminated a spiritual teaching, expressed through the special symbolism of the cards. Some historians say that mystic Sufi sects from Persia and India were responsible for the introduction of symbolism to tarot. Issues of fate, death and resurrection, rebirth and reincarnation were passed on to even the illiterate through such cards as Death, the Devil, the Last Judgement, the World and the Stars. The combination of Gypsy mystique and tarot images affects all who come into contact with them.

In the late nineteenth century many commentators on existing tarot decks and designers of new tarots attributed the symbolism to the Jewish mystical system of the Kabbala, by linking the Hebrew alphabet of 22 letters to the major arcana cards, and the four suits to the letters of the Tetragrammaton, the hidden name of God YHVH (yod, heh, vau, heh). In some decks the figures in the major arcana were represented in positions which echoed the shape of the Hebrew letters.

Archetypal Symbolism

It may be asked how medieval symbols have retained their power for so many centuries, despite concerted efforts to eradicate them. The answer is that tarot cards contain archetypal images which awaken non-rational memories buried within us – the inner world of symbols we all possess. Archetypes are behaviour patterns which are ingrained in the psyche of all humans, transmitted through the common genetic inheritance of our ancestors back to the cave and before. Civilization tames and formalizes basic instincts such as hunger, sexuality, possessiveness, jealousy, defensiveness, aggression and territorialism into conventional behaviour – but all these urges remain within us, awaiting those times when circumstances force them into expression despite the control of our conscious mind. Our instinctual reality contains archetypal patterns, carried by symbols that, although cryptic to our conscious mind, communicate clearly with our unconscious. The deep psychological patterns which we all share are called the *collective unconscious*, as distinct from the personal unconscious, which are the repressed memories and instincts from our childhood. The symbols of tarot cards communicate directly with our unconscious mind, heart and soul in such a way that they bypass the censors of consciousness, which regard such images as primitive, childish, infantile or regressive. Tarot cards are directed at the archetypal level of reality, an especially powerful experience for twentieth century women and men. We have become separated from our roots, and this is reflected in our abuse of other humans and of the earth itself.

How may these archetypal images be used and what is the intention of tarot? The sequence of cards is often likened to the unfolding process of the psyche in its quest for unity with the universe. The cards aid the psyche to focus, concentrate and guide energy. The series of images depicted by the cards link our psyche with the process of initiation. As initiates we start anew each time we question our direction or seek a higher level of awareness and understanding.

Chapter 1

THE
MANDALA
ASTROLOGICAL
TAROT

The Mandala Astrological Tarot is a unique synthesis of classical tarot designs presented as circular mandala images, and organized by astrology.

Historical tarot cards carry many layers of meaning illustrated in a pictorial, symbolic language. Among the significant symbol systems encoded in the cards are mythology, colours, numbers, astrological signs and planets, Hebrew letters, animals, plants, personifications, geometrical patterns, architecture, landscapes and man-made objects. The symbols on the cards lead the tarot reader or meditator to discover many layers of meaning.

Although the traditional tarot iconography is medieval, there are and always have been traces of symbols from earlier cultures, as well as additions by more recent commentators and illustrators. The vitality and power of tarot is largely due to the collision of images that come from medieval Christianity with those from more primal eras, particularly from the Egyptians, Chaldeans, Greeks and Romans. In those cultures many gods and goddesses were worshipped at the same time, as distinct from the later religions of one god. But Christianized medieval images carry the gods and goddesses within them.

Often the same image serves to remind us of a series of archetypal figures. The trump of the High Priestess has been called the Papess by some because of the legendary ninth century Pope Joan, but was earlier associated with Mary Magdalene, the moon goddess Luna, the Triple Goddess, Juno, the huntress Diana, or the goddess of wisdom, Sophia. Similarly, the trump of the Magician is based upon the ibis-headed Egyptian god Thoth, creator and organizer of the universe, inventor of hieroglyphs, the arts and sciences, and also the god of the dead and lord of karma. The Magician is also known as Hermes Trismegistus (Thrice-Greatest Hermes) and as the Roman god Mercury. The healer and magician Hermes carried a staff of entwined snakes. His feminine counterpart is the goddess Maat, the incarnation of truth symbolized by her ostrich feather diadem, who accompanied Thoth at the weighing of souls in the Egyptian mysteries. The major arcana cards carry archetypal and godlike levels of meaning which have a particular appeal and great power in our godless days.

The mythology of tarot is capable of being interpreted in any number of ways. In the mythological origin and meaning of the major arcana cards it is posssible to see traces of the suppressed worship of the matriarchal Great Goddess. Within the context of humanistic or depth psychology there is a mythological simplicity and accessibility about the cards which may be used in conjunction with psychotherapy or psychoanalysis as keys or guides to the archetypal experiential journey.

In using tarot cards with their psychological and historical roots, the individual questing after deeper understanding of the life process and an opportunity for meditation, has access to a library of the spiritual quest of humanity.

The Mandala Astrological Tarot differs primarily from traditional decks because there are no human images. In most tarot decks the arcana are illustrated by personifications of the Emperor, Hermit or Hanged Man, while in a card such as the World there is a veiled and androgynous woman, centrally located and floating in space. The only three cards in which there are no human figures are the Wheel of Fortune and the Moon, in both of which there are animal figures, and Death, in which there is a skeleton. Otherwise, each card has a figure with which the initiate identifies and upon which a stage of development or query is projected.

According to tradition, the tarot major arcana are stages of initiation into the ancient Egyptian mysteries. Within the sacred precincts of the Egyptian temple, there was a great hall with 22 pairs of columns framing tableaux which illustrated the 22 stages of initiation. Between each pair of columns there was a scene of an appropriate landscape complete with correct colours, ritual objects, animals and images, also containing the necessary implements to alter the symbolic identity of the initiate. There were costumes and wigs to wear, weapons or magical implements to carry, and ritual poses to adopt. A residue of this ceremonial may still be seen in Masonic rituals. When the identification was complete, the initiate would move on to the next stage of the process. The entire initiation could take hours, days or years according to the understanding, experience and inclination of the initiate.

The initiate, directed by the High Priest, was led through the stages within the temple, taught about the correct images, ideas, principles and sounds appropriate to the stage, and then required to enter the tableaux and adopt the role of, for example, the Empress, Hermit or Strength.

The images of the Mandala Astrological Tarot are the tableaux of the

X WHEEL OF FORTUNE KAPH ⊃   XVIII   MOON   QOPH ק   XIII   DEATH   NUN נ

♐♓ PISCES SAGITTARIUS JUPITER CANCER ♋   ♃ ♆ NEPTUNE JUPITER PISCES VENUS ♀   ♂ ♇ PLUTO MARS SCORPIO URANUS ♅

Egyptian mystery temples with all the appropriate scenery, imagery, colours and textures, symbolic costumes and ritual implements, so that you, as the initiate, may step into each role in the course of a tarot reading or in meditating upon the images.

Mandala

Mandala is an Eastern term for a consecrated place, a map of the cosmos or a geometric projection of the world reduced to an essential pattern. A meditator uses a mandala to identify with the forces of the universe and to collect their power. Mandala images bring heavenly essence down into manifestation. A mandala is a reflection of the universe, often with representations of the gods and their abodes clearly positioned upon it.

The classic form of the mandala is like a circular unfolded lotus flower, symbolic of creation as it blossoms upon the celestial waters. The mandala is a support for meditation, an external instrument to provoke and procure internal visions of the godhead. By using mandalas, the meditator can concentrate the mind and rediscover the way to reach the secret inner reality.

The mandala is, above all, a diagram of concentric circles, a protected space within which images of the archetypal world of paradise are represented as an ideal landscape such as the holy Mount Meru or the ideal city.

The Mandala Astrological Tarot presents each tarot card as a mandala image – circular images upon square cards. Each card may be placed with any one of its four sides to the top because each side refers to one of the cardinal orientations. The images are traditional variations, but the symbols are displayed centrally and the positions of all landscape details, ritual instruments and other symbols are determined by their meaning within the whole. Meditation upon any card is not only a way to discover its inner meaning, but also a way to contact your own psychic centre.

The major arcana cards contain many images arranged in mandala format, as though they were ideal images of the perfect world of archetypes. Each card leads from the periphery to the centre, wherein balance reigns, just as in the human psyche. The form of the cards is conducive to wholeness.

The square shape of the cards is very important. Typical tarot cards are rectangular like playing cards. Since the card images have a top and bottom, many commentators describe the meaning of each card in its upright position as positive and when reversed as negative. Since the process of enlightenment is centrally concerned with eliminating the distinction between positive and negative, as indeed all pairs of oppositions, to value the card in this way is essentially dualistic. The square cards provide a solution to this dilemma.

The four cardinal orientations at any location are above, below, right and left. The astrological significance of these cardinal positions provide qualifications for the tarot card meanings.

A card in the upright position shows one conscious of the quality described. If the Fool, indicating innocence is upright it implies one who is not only innocent, but knows that he is innocent.

A card in the upside down position is unconscious of its quality. The reversed Fool would be someone who was innocent but unaware of being so, and therefore truly a fool.

When the upper title of a card is to the left, toward the eastern horizon where the sun rises, the quality of the card is carried in the personality and acted out. Thus the Fool in this position would be one who acts like an innocent.

When the title of a card is to the right, toward the western horizon where the sun sets, the quality of the card is derived from, or a projection on to, someone else in the outside world, such as one's partner.

Each card therefore has not just one, but four meanings based upon its position. The symbols and images of each card also change position, creating many permutations of all cards in the deck. Although this is a degree of subtlety which is not required in the beginning, it provides great depth and accuracy later on in your use of the Mandala Astrological Tarot.

The Astrological Structure of Tarot

Astrology is probably the oldest symbolic language for expressing the processes of life in nature, as well as of our human existence from cradle to grave. Although many tarot commentators through the ages have ascribed correspondences between major arcana cards and the signs and planets, the astrological structure underlying tarot has rarely been presented clearly or

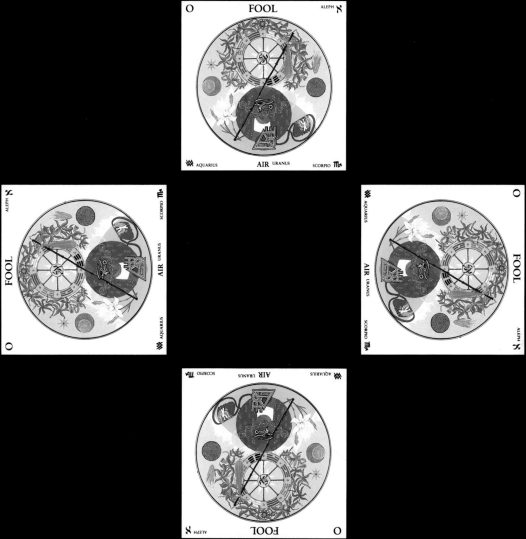

completely. The greatest advantage of the synthesis of tarot and astrology in the Mandala Astrological Tarot is that using the two symbol systems together allows a greater depth of interpretation, and the numbered minor arcana cards and the court cards may be connected to the major arcana.

The 22 major arcana cards are divided into three groups, corresponding to the 12 signs of the zodiac, the seven planets and three elements. The attributions are as follows:

The Three Elements

Air	O	Fool
Water	XII	Hanged Man
Fire (Spirit)	XX	Judgement

The Seven Planets

Mercury	I	Magician
Moon	II	High Priestess
Venus	III	Empress
Jupiter	X	Wheel of Fortune
Mars	XVI	Tower
Sun	XIX	Sun
Saturn	XXI	World

The Twelve Signs of the Zodiac

Aries	IV	Emperor
Taurus	V	High Priest
Gemini	VI	Lovers
Cancer	VII	Chariot
Leo	VIII	Fortitude
Virgo	IX	Hermit
Libra	XI	Justice
Scorpio	XIII	Death
Sagittarius	XIV	Temperance
Capricorn	XV	Devil
Aquarius	XVII	Stars
Pisces	XVIII	Moon

The missing fourth element, Earth, is not represented by an individual card but is the entire major arcana itself – an expression of the visible and tangible universe.

The major arcana cards can be described by their atrological significance as well as by their traditional tarot archetypes. The action of each of the three categories is quite different, and all three are required to structure the world. In using tarot cards the following levels of action are very important.

The three elements are pure primal qualities or causes which motivate the world, and from which the more individual qualities of planets and the signs emanate. Spirit is created by God from out of the void; from spirit emanates air as the vehicle of the word; from air is extracted primordial water. In the Hebrew Kabbala, the elements are the three Mothers from which the world evolves.

The seven planets are the heavens, following next in the sequence of creation, representing the divine archetypes as cyclic mechanisms and ways of action. The seven are solar systems, earths, continents, seas, deserts, days of the week, notes in the musical scale and colours in the spectrum. In the Kabbala they are double letters, each of which can be pronounced in two different ways, symbolizing their duality, their softness and hardness, their strength and weakness. They symbolize the qualities of wisdom, riches, fertility, life, power, peace and grace, and their opposites.

The 12 signs of the zodiac are stages of the unfolding of the year and of the evolution of spirit through a complete cycle. They are the fundamental properties of life as manifest ways of being, parts of the body and months in the year. In the Kabbala, the 12 simple letters symbolize the zodiac signs correlated to fundamental properties such as speech, thought, movement, sight, hearing, work, coition, smell, sleep, anger, taste and mirth.

The combinations of elements, planets and signs describe all actions in the physical world, all possible permutations of behaviour, and therefore provide a perfect symbol system or vocabulary for divination.

The great advantage of attributing the tarot cards directly to elements, planets and signs is that their combinations are already the subject of the science and art of astrology. When the cards Empress and Emperor are chosen together in a reading, apart from the obvious significance of a meeting of powerful female and male, they can be seen as the planet Venus (Empress) in the sign Aries (Emperor), which is astrologically interpreted as a self-centred relationship or an ardent demonstration of affection.

The four suits of the court cards and the minor arcana correspond to the four elements, fire, air, water and earth, which in turn correspond to Platonic bodies, psychological functions (according to Jung) and series of astrological signs.

Tarot Suit	Wands	Swords	Cups	Pentacles
Element	Fire	Air	Water	Earth
Card Suit	Clubs	Spades	Hearts	Diamonds
Body	Spirit	Mind	Emotion	Body
Function	Intuition	Thinking	Feeling	Sensation
Astrology	Wands	Swords	Cups	Pentacles
Cardinal Queen	Aries	Libra	Cancer	Capricorn
Fixed King	Leo	Aquarius	Scorpio	Taurus
Mutable Prince	Sagittarius	Gemini	Pisces	Virgo

The Personal Planets

☉ **Sun**　Spirit, consciousness, individuality, masculine principle, dignity, honour. Man, father, authoritative figure.

☾ **Moon**　Soul, unconscious, personality, instinct, emotions, fertility. Woman, mother, wife, the nation, the church.

☿ **Mercury**　Mind, reason, self-expression, communication, knowledge, intelligence, movement. Friend, sibling, mediator, guide.

♀ **Venus**　Love, beauty, art, social life, harmony, integration, attraction. Young woman, lover, mistress, artist.

♂ **Mars**　Will, desire, energy, enthusiasm, temper, arrogance, passion. Young man, fighter, athlete, craftsman.

♃ **Jupiter**　Idealism, vision, expansion, mania, success, popularity, religion. Philosopher, psychologist, guru, the wealthy.

♄ **Saturn**　Reality, pragmatism, contraction, depression, definition, concentration, organization. Business person, economist, merchant, miner.

The Collective Planets

♅ **Uranus**　Altruism, originality, independence, inspiration, abstraction. Individualist, inventor, eccentric, rebel, revolutionary.

♆ **Neptune**　Divinity, idealism, spirituality, dreamlife, clairvoyance, sensitivity. Medium, psychic, musician, addict.

♇ **Pluto**　Power, the masses, magic, propaganda, force, force majeure, frankness. Politician, actor, magician.

☊ **Moon's Node**　Community, family, alliance, adaptability, the astral. Relative, groupy, friend, associate.

The symbol system from which the planetary glyphs evolved is also prominent throughout tarot imagery. All planetary glyphs are composed of combinations of three basic forms:

The Circle – representing pure Spirit
The Half-Circle or Crescent – representing Soul
The Cross – representing Matter or Body

Each planet is a combination of these three symbols.

The Sun is pure spirit concentrated, as shown by the dot in the centre of the circle. The Moon is a half-circle or crescent, showing her reflective and dualistic qualities. The Earth is a cross of matter within a circle. Venus is spirit elevated above matter, while Mars is a corrupt representation of the cross of matter elevated above spirit. Mercury is three-fold, with the circle of spirit as a mediator between soul above and matter below. Jupiter is soul elevated above matter, while Saturn is matter above soul.

The collective or generational planets are more complex. Uranus is spirit

surmounted by a cross between two crescents as spirit transformed by conditioned matter. Neptune is a crescent speared above the cross of matter. Pluto is spirit dominating matter through the mediation of the soul.

The symbols of the planets are particularly important in the Mandala Astrological Tarot because they form the basis for many of the images. In place of figures such as the Empress or Emperor, feminine figures are shown as either the Venus (♀) or the Moon (☾) glyph, while masculine figures are shown as either the Mars symbol (♂) or the Sun (☉). The Mercury glyph (☿) represents the combination of male and female, spirit and soul. The glyphs for the Sun and Moon appear in many cards in a variety of positions, showing their relative meaning. The planetary glyphs are coloured, adorned and placed in the appropriate landscape as are their equivalent personalities.

Another symbol which appears in some of the major arcana such as the Hanged Man, the Universe, the Emperor and the Wheel of Fortune, is the triangle surmounting the cross, the alchemical symbol of sulphur (♁). Sulphur is the substance from which all others came into being, a universal solvent and a symbol for the enlightened being. The symbol is the element fire elevated above matter.

The relative positions of such symbols in the cards are very significant and represent deeper layers of meaning available to those willing to meditate upon the cards.

The Signs of the Zodiac

♈ **Aries the Ram**   21 Mar–20 Apr.
Cardinal, Masculine, Fire Sign
Germinating times; unfolding energy; self-assertion; initiatory energy;
adventure; daring; impatience; enterprising.

♉ **Taurus the Bull**   21 Apr–20 May
Fixed, Feminine, Earth Sign
Invigorating and strengthening; form creation; preservation; the physical
world; the senses; matter; fertility; security; finances; stewardship.

♊ **Gemini the Twins**   21 May–20 Jun
Mutable, Masculine, Air Sign
Diversity; multiplication; vitality; adaptability. Instinctive mind; imitation;
communication; duality; versatility; mobility; intelligence.

♋ **Cancer the Crab**   21 Jun–22 Jul
Cardinal, Feminine, Water Sign
Mothering; fecundation; fertilization. Feeling; emotions; mother; home and
family; the unconscious; protective urge; possessiveness.

♌ **Leo the Lion**   23 Jul–23 Aug
Fixed, Masculine, Fire Sign
Ripening; summer heat; full energy; extroversion; harvest.
Power; self-expression; personal love; games; pleasure; ruling; vanity;
proudness.

♍ **Virgo the Virgin**   24 Aug–22 Sep
Mutable, Feminine, Earth Sign
Ripe fruit; orderly storage and collection; selection. Discrimination; purity;
perfectionism; health and hygiene; analytic mind; prudence; diet.

♎ **Libra the Balance**   23 Sep–22 Oct
Cardinal, Masculine, Air Sign
Balance and adjustment; thanksgiving; social persuasion; balancing.
Partnership; marriage; public relations; enemies; sublimation; yielding.

♏ **Scorpio the Scorpion**   23 Oct–22 Nov
Fixed, Feminine, Water Sign
Death of vegetation; life of the seed; survival; endurance. Regeneration;
passion; separation; emotional intensity; dependency; losses; inheritance;
the occult.

♐ **Sagittarius the Centaur**   23 Nov–21 Dec
Mutable, Masculine, Fire Sign
Hibernation; advent; the inner life; meditation; expansion. Realization;
aspiration; higher mind; religion and philosophy; sport; freedom; rebirth.

♑ **Capricorn the Goat**   22 Dec – 19 Jan
Cardinal, Feminine, Earth Sign
Preservation; patience; reality; self-concentration. Perfected matter; ego
objectives; organization; power and success; position; government.

♒ **Aquarius the Waterbearer**   20 Jan – 19 Feb
Fixed, Masculine, Air Sign
Waiting; fasting; Lent; observation and planning. Abstraction; conscience;
humanitarian; detached; coldness; utopian; altruism; scientific.

♓ **Pisces the Fishes**   20 Feb – 20 Mar
Mutable, Feminine, Water Sign
Swelling seed; purifying rain; serenity; potential. Sensitivity; destiny;
receptivity; self-sacrifice; psychic impulse; karma; seclusion; mysticism.

Each zodiacal sign has one or two planets which rule it. The ruling planets
work particularly well through the sign and have an affinity with it. For
example, the fiery and energetic Sun rules Leo, the sign of extrovert, positive
behaviour. Some planets rule two signs in which they act most archetypally in
an active or passive way. Mercury rules the positive sign Gemini and the
passive sign Virgo. Venus rules the positive Libra and the passive Taurus.
The rulerships give additional qualities for interpretation. Each planet is also
exalted in a sign in which it is most powerful. The Sun, which rules Leo, is
exalted in Aries where it supports self-assertion.

Sun rules *Leo* and is exalted in *Aries*.
Moon rules *Cancer* and is exalted in *Taurus*.
Mercury rules *Gemini* and *Virgo* and is exalted in *Virgo*.
Venus rules *Taurus* and *Libra* and is exalted in *Pisces*.
Mars rules *Aries* and *Scorpio* and is exalted in *Capricorn*.
Jupiter rules *Sagittarius* and *Pisces* and is exalted in *Cancer*.
Saturn rules *Capricorn* and *Aquarius* and is exalted in *Libra*.
Uranus rules *Aquarius* and is exalted in *Scorpio*.
Neptune rules *Pisces* and is exalted in *Cancer*.
Pluto rules *Scorpio* and is exalted in *Leo*.

For example, the major arcana card Strength is the card associated with the
sign Leo, implying personal strength and self-expression. At the bottom left
of the card is the ruler Sun and at the right the exaltation Pluto. Strength
therefore contains qualities not only of Leo, but of the Sun and Pluto as well.
A trump associated with a zodiac sign has the planet or planets which rule
and are exalted in it at the bottom of the card. A trump associated with a
planet shows the sign or signs which it rules and exalts. The three trumps
associated with the elements are co-ruled by an outer planet, either Uranus,
Neptune or Pluto. The Fool is associated with the element Air and Uranus.
The Hanged Man is associated with the element Water and Neptune.
The Judgement is associated with the element Fire and Pluto.
The major arcana cards have associations with signs and planets, and in

some cases signs, planets and elements. Their multiple attributions are symbolic of the importance and complexity of the trumps.

Colour Symbolism

The spectrum of colours is a rainbow bridge connecting the spiritual to the physical world. The seven colours appear when light passes through a prism. White contains all the colours of the spectrum and black is the absence of colour. On the very simplest and most subjective level, the three primary colours red, yellow and blue were seen to represent the qualities of force, intelligence and consciousness. For example, the Hindu god Vishnu is depicted as having blue skin, signifying his holiness and divinity. Red is hot, lusty, passionate, fiery and is correlated with instinctive actions, warlike attitudes and excessive irrationality, and in medieval times was identified with the inferno and the Devil. Yellow is associated with the Sun as a spiritual source of energy which is life-sustaining, fruitful and good. In the early printed tarot decks the only colours were red, blue and yellow, and the symbolism was therefore simple to decode. The intermediate colours were given qualities which corresponded with their places in nature, so that, for example, the green of plants was youthful, fecund and lush.

Colours were associated with the planets from the earliest times. The red planet Mars carries warlike energy, the silvery moon is reflective, illusory and magical, and the ever-changing white-yellow Mercury is rapid, elusive and bright. The greenish morning and evening star Venus holds sway over lovers because the ancients considered the times just after sunset and just before sunrise as the best times to make love. The watery but brilliant Jupiter signified celestial wisdom and the religious impulse, while the violet Saturn was envisioned as icy cold, the master of death. Again, the attributions were primarily subjective, and based on observation.

The seven major planets correspond to the seven colours of the spectrum.

Planets	Colour
Sun	orange and gold
Moon	indigo, silver and white
Mercury	yellow
Venus	green
Mars	red
Jupiter	blue
Saturn	violet

Since the three outer, collective planets Uranus, Neptune and Pluto are considered the higher octaves of the planets Mercury, Venus and Mars, their colours are correlated.

Uranus	pale yellow
Neptune	pale green
Pluto	pale red

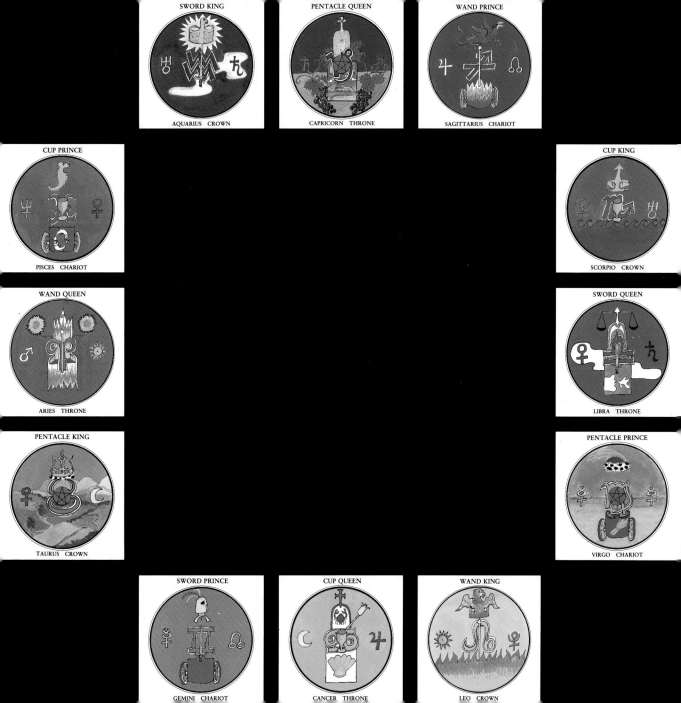

SWORD KING
AQUARIUS CROWN

PENTACLE QUEEN
CAPRICORN THRONE

WAND PRINCE
SAGITTARIUS CHARIOT

CUP PRINCE
PISCES CHARIOT

CUP KING
SCORPIO CROWN

WAND QUEEN
ARIES THRONE

SWORD QUEEN
LIBRA THRONE

PENTACLE KING
TAURUS CROWN

PENTACLE PRINCE
VIRGO CHARIOT

SWORD PRINCE
GEMINI CHARIOT

CUP QUEEN
CANCER THRONE

WAND KING
LEO CROWN

The most interesting and logical manner of colour attribution is to correlate the succession of colours of the spectrum from red to violet to the 12 signs of the zodiac from Aries to Pisces. The correspondences satisfy ancient instinctive qualities and in addition are accurate in regard to planetary significance. The specific colouration used in the Mandala Astrological Tarot is the King Scale of colour, which utilizes the following attributions:

Zodiac signs	Colour	Ruling planet
Aries	red	Mars
Taurus	red-orange	
Gemini	orange	Mercury
Cancer	yellow-orange	
Leo	yellow	Sun
Virgo	yellow-green	
Libra	green	Venus
Scorpio	blue-green	
Sagittarius	blue	Jupiter
Capricorn	indigo	
Aquarius	violet	Saturn
Pisces	red-violet	

The last sign Pisces completes the zodiacal circle, and is therefore the transitional colour red-violet which makes the transition back to the beginning of the spectrum. The planets which rule the positive fire and air signs correlate with their appropriate signs, although the Sun and Mercury switch places – the Sun is more usually attributed to either orange or gold and Mercury to yellow, but they are never more than one sign apart in the sky. Through the King Scale the gradation of colours corresponds to the gradual process of humanization, abstraction and civilization to which the successive zodiac signs refer as well. The primal and animalistic red gradually vibrates much more slowly than the finer violet. Green is the central colour of balance, midway through the spectrum as its counterpart Libra is the intermediary zodiac sign.

Wrapping the spectrum around the zodiacal circle pays unexpected dividends which are aesthetically pleasing, mathematically satisfactory and magical. Magic in its truest sense is the evocation of the reality behind appearances. Each primary colour has an isomorphic opposite, and these pairs are positioned opposite each other around the circle, so that opposite signs have opposite colours. Thus the instinctive and aggressive red of Aries and its ruling planet Mars is in opposition to and complements the sedate and fecund green of Libra and its ruling planet Venus. The energy of the life principle expressed in the orange of Gemini is in opposition to the reasoned and philosophical meditative calm of Sagittarius and its ruling planet Jupiter. The fiery and egocentric creativity of yellow Leo and its ruling planet the Sun is opposite the detached, abstract and spiritual violet of Aquarius and its ruling planet Saturn.

SWORD NINE

VENUS   GEMINI

The Mandala Astrological Tarot uses the King Scale to bring the colour representation of the court cards and the minor arcana into correspondence with the much more elaborate and complex major arcana. The 12 Kings, Queens and Princes have backgrounds coloured to correspond to their appropriate astrological signs; when they are placed around a circle in their correct zodiacal order, they illustrate the complete colour spectrum in the circle.

The minor arcana cards correlate with thirds of each sign, the decanates, and are coloured according to the sign and planet acting in the sign. The central circle is the colour of the sign, and the outer ring is the colour of the ruling planet of the decanate. For example, the Sword Nine corresponds to the second decanate of Gemini, ruled by Venus, therefore the central circle of the card is the orange of Gemini surrounded by the green of Venus.

As will be seen, when complex reading layouts are used, this system makes it easy to see which cards are related to each other.

Tarot Symbols

It is important to understand some of the basic symbols of the language of the tarot. The commonest symbols are derived from architecture, plants, animals, postures and crafted objects.

The pair of columns between which many of the tarot archetypes are placed represents the structure of the world, and may be understood as metaphors for the way the world is seen. Our own world view is always compared to the real world. Sometimes the columns are black and white, symbolizing the dualism of inside and outside, us and them, and the forces of life and death, male and female, good and bad, left and right sides of the brain, conscious and unconscious. When the pair of columns is arched it represents a gateway into and out of the world of form. When four columns are shown they represent the four elements which create or support the physical universe.

The canopy of stars is symbolic of the influence of astrology or the astral sphere.

The cube is symbolic of the four elements, as well as being earth. Square shapes represent the four elements, the earth or physical reality.

The triangle represents the active trinity comprising birth, death and rebirth or the three Platonic physical, emotional and mental bodies. An upward pointing triangle is the element fire and the resolution of duality by a higher third point, while a downward pointing triangle is the element water, and the tendency to sink into the unconscious. An upward pointing triangle bisected by a horizontal line is the element air, while a downward pointing triangle bisected by a horizontal line is the element earth. Upward and downward triangles intersecting create the Seal of Solomon, the integration of physical and spiritual worlds, and contain all four triangular elements.

Stars either represent actual constellations which are symbolic, such as the zodiac signs, the Pleiades or Sirius, or are bodies encasing spirit, mind and soul. In esoteric astrology, seven stars represent the seven solar systems from which the present world was evolved, acting through the Seven Sisters or the Great Bear.

The horizontal figure 8 is the symbol of infinity, also called the lemniscate, which is the sign of the holy spirit.

Keys are symbolic of the secret doctrine, and gold and silver keys signify male and female qualities.

The spherical orb is a symbol of worldly power, yet has the connotation of spirituality when surmounted by a cross, which is associated with papal dominance.

The arrow is symbolic of will, spirit or fire.

The heart is love, the seat of the soul and divine suffering.

The eye or third eye is the available higher centre within the spiritual domain of humanity.

The crown is dominion, royal position and high status. The triple crown symbolizes the integration of, or power over, the physical, emotional and spiritual bodies.

The pyramid is the resolution of the physical world (the four sides) in a higher, transcendent state (the apex).

Many of the symbols of tarot are animals, insects or plants.

The snake is a symbol of time and infinity when forming two tangential circles. When a snake bites its own tail it becomes the ouroburos, and symbolizes the eternal return, the cyclic nature of the world and beginning and end. The hooded cobra is a holy Egyptian symbol of power over time; it is also an Indian symbol of time as the river of life, and as a naga, the cobra which spread its hood over Buddha during his enlightenment.

The caduceus is a wand intertwined by two snakes, which signifies the union of the left and right sides of the brain, of soul and spirit, and is the classic sign of the medical profession.

Corn is symbolic of fertility and plenty, as well as of the ritual fertilization, death and renewal of the Grain Goddess.

Roses are associated with love and lovers, and as mystic symbols of the heart.

The sunflower moves with the sun and is solar and masculine.

The dog is loyal instinct, faithfulness, stewardship, and is often associated with the underworld as a guardian.

The eagle is justice, temporal power, majesty and strength. Hawks are solar and represent transformation, being related to the Egyptian solar god Osiris. Eagle or hawk wings astride a solar disk are emblems of the sun god and the spiritual principle.

The phoenix is often confused with the eagle, but it has a mythic meaning of rebirth for upon being destroyed by fire, it is reborn instantly from the ashes.

The crane is a symbol of justice and wisdom, and is the image of Thoth Hermes.

Bees and butterflies are symbolic of the soul, rebirth and the eternal life.

Crabs, lobsters or crayfish are symbolic of the emergence of humanity from the unconscious sea, and of the fertilizing potential of water.

Natural forces were worshipped from earliest times and remain potent symbols.

Mountains are the quest, resolution, meditation, being "above it all" and symbolic of higher realms of the Self.

Lightning is inspiration, direct communication from the gods, intuition and divine intercession.

The cornfield is fertility and the manifest principle of love.

Barren landscapes are devoid of love and affection, and are often considered Saturnine and cold.

Trees are symbolic of the process of evolution and integration according to the manner of their branching. In ancient times trees were regarded as sacred spirits and worshipped. The dying or barren tree is negative life.

The Composition of the Cards

The symbols of tarot are combined within each major arcana card to present a meaning which is directly perceived by the unconscious and has a powerful effect there, whether or not the conscious mind can understand the meaning of the symbol.

The relative position of the specific symbols of each card is also very important in the Mandala Astrological Tarot. The primary geometric divisions of the cards describe the area in which a particular symbol is active, as is the case in all mandala diagrams. The primary divisions are a reflection of the places around the astrological horoscope as seasons of the year and times of the day.

The primary division is into upper and lower halves. The upper half is the conscious, objective and masculine domain of the sun, while the lower half is the unconscious, subjective and feminine domain of the moon. The symbolism of the sun travelling across the sky and down through the underworld at night led to myths of the sun as a charioteer, and the yearly cycle of vegetation apparently disappearing into the earth was at the core of the ancient mysteries of life and death.

The secondary division of the circle is into right and left halves. In mandala symbolism the right side is instinctive, artistic, intuitive and holistic, while the left side is linear, logical, analytical, mathematical, verbal and concrete. Astrologically, the left side is the domain of the personality and the right side is the not-self or the outside world. Modern brain research has proved that there is a crossover: the left side of the brain governs the right side of the body, and the right side of the brain governs the left side of the body. This is symbolized esoterically by the rainbow bridge or the caduceus symbol of Mercury, which governs the corpus callosum or neural bridge crossing over from one half to the other.

The Kabbala

The correlation of the Hebrew mystical system of the Kabbala with tarot is theoretically medieval, although there is little evidence to support a direct connection. The most obvious correlation is that there are 22 major arcana cards and 22 letters in the Hebrew alphabet. Each Hebrew letter has a symbol, a numerical value and a direct meaning, the subject of many exhaustive books. A primary structure in Hebrew mysticism is the tenfold Tree of Life, a structure which features prominently in the Mandala Astrological Tarot. Between the 10 energy centres (sephira) on the tree are 22 paths – the combination of the 10 numbers and the 22 paths creates the entire universe of form, just as the 22 major arcana and the sets of 10 minor arcana describe all archetypal patterns.

A factor which supports the connection is the division of the Hebrew alphabet into three groups of letters which define the tarot cards very clearly. This is the division into three mothers, seven doubles and 12 simples, which relate clearly to the three elements, seven planets and 12 signs as we have previously seen.

The three mother letters are primordial, spiritual and are the sounds of breath:

a aleph	primordial air	air	Fool
m mem	primordial water	water	Hanged Man
sh shin	primordial fire	fire	Judgement

The seven double letters emanating from the mother are dual; strong and weak:

b beth	power	Mercury	Magician
g gimel	wisdom	Moon	High Priestess
d daleth	life	Venus	Empress
k kaph	grace	Jupiter	Wheel of Fortune
p peh	riches	Mars	Tower
r resh	fertility	Sun	Sun
t tau	peace	Saturn	World

The 12 simple letters emanating from the doubles are fundamental properties:

h heh	speech	Aries	Emperor
v vau	thought	Taurus	High Priest
z zain	movement	Gemini	Lovers
ch cheth	sight	Cancer	Chariot
t teth	hearing	Leo	Strength
y yod	work	Virgo	Hermit
l lamed	coition	Libra	Justice
n nun	smell	Scorpio	Death
s samekh	sleep	Sagittarius	Temperance
o ayin	anger	Capricorn	Devil
tz tzaddi	taste	Aquarius	Star
q qoph	mirth	Pisces	Moon

The letters of the Hebrew alphabet may be arranged in many numerical sequences which show the emanation of spiritual being into manifestation. As an art of divination, there are also ways of adding up the numbers which correspond to each card so that the meanings of similar phrases or combinations of letters may be correlated. All words composed of letters which add up to the same total have related meanings.

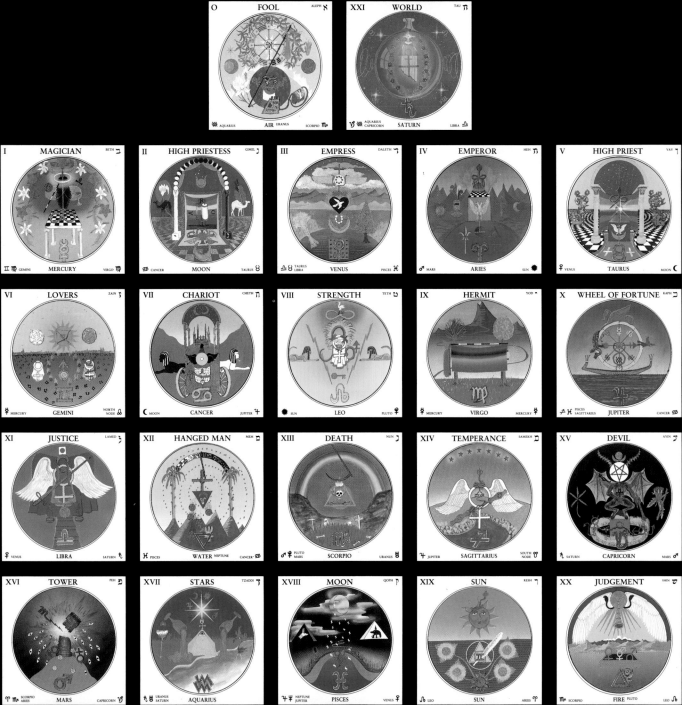

Chapter 2

THE
MAJOR
ARCANA

The 22 major arcana cards, from the unnumbered Fool to the Universe describe the process of enlightenment. Although the sequence of cards is not to be taken literally as consecutive phases of an actual initiation, there is much to be learned by becoming familiar with the cards and their images, pondering why the order is as it is, and, perhaps most important, generally becoming comfortable with the symbolic language of the psyche.

The major arcana are special cards because they have the most layers of meaning, are less easy to define and the richest in symbolism. The heart of our being does not want to be right or to know, but rather to be. Our personality wishes to identify with what we are now, what we could be in the future, or what we were in the past, but all these states are temporary and lead us away from our centre. With regular use, care and understanding, tarot can lead to a state higher than any pictured in the cards, when the process itself is brought inside. One could almost say that at that level the cards themselves become extraneous because they exist inside more vividly than they do outside. This is the state of being.

Every person has distinctive qualities, likes and dislikes, certain idiosyncrasies and an appearance which characterizes them throughout life. The mask of personality may change gradually with age, but the outer appearances are always a compensation for the true reality within. It must be understood and felt that the intention of tarot is to invoke the will to investigate, experience and acknowledge those cards which at first sight seem to be least clear. In order to be free, it is essential to integrate shadow qualities which seem evil or dark, to accept all the parts which do not seem to fit easily and above all to allow the existence of all facets of the whole. In the complete being all parts need expression. Tarot is a wonderful learning tool for the accomplishment of this aim.

THE FOOL

Number O
The element Air and the planet Uranus
Aleph is balance

The Traditional Fool

The Fool is the beginning and the end. Some decks place the Fool before the other 21 cards and others place him last. Ambiguity is shown by his number, which is zero, although in some decks he is unnumbered. A youth starts out on a quest with boundless confidence, carrying a small bag containing all his worldly possessions and accompanied by a small dog. He is dressed in a fool's cap and pays no heed to the barking of the dog, who sees that his master is about to walk off the brink of a precipice, representing the world. He is full of confidence and enthusiasm and can become anything, like youth embarking into adult life.

The Symbolism of the Fool

The Fool is governed by the element Air, indicating the dominance of mind to which our being is entrusted in the world. That the mind is often erratic and unpredictable is indicated by the co-ruler Uranus. The circular jacket embroidered with magical symbols and the wheel of fortune above form an infinity symbol showing that even with purity and the enthusiasm of youth, the world changes continually and we must adjust to it – the end of one issue is the beginning of the next. His bag of possessions contains the elements, except for the sword of discrimination, which hold the key to his fate, showing that outer appearances are often misleading in relation to the essence within. The sun at the right and moon at the left show the necessary combination of male and female qualities in everyone.

Divination Meanings

Awakening perception. Dominance of thoughts which contradict reality. Folly. Enthusiasm and naivete of youth. Immaturity. Irrationality. Beginning an adventure. Neglecting details. Taking the initiative without considering the consequences. Being guided by intuition.

Reversed Meanings

Foolishness. Getting into trouble. Being unaware of the consequences of starting an action.

O   FOOL   ALEPH א

AQUARIUS   AIR URANUS   SCORPIO ♏

MAGICIAN

Number I
The planet Mercury
Beth is power

The Traditional Magician

The master Magician manipulates the elements, juggling them in the air and balancing their antagonistic energies, showing the possibility of guiding the archetypes. The number one is unity, the whole, the origin from which the other numbers arise. The winged god Hermes is the model, the creator and organizer of the physical universe, and contains the power to focus, concentrate and direct energy and mind to achieve creation – this is true magic. The wig of appearances hides the essence, but the Magician penetrates duality.

The Symbolism of the Magician

The Magician is governed by Mercury, the planet of instinctive mind which may either be discriminating in Virgo or adaptable and versatile in Gemini. Orange is purified mind. The double-ended wand, the duality of the physical world, is the focus of the balancing trick and only touches the physical plane at one point, the intersection of the ouroburos snake – the mind is precise but its effects are not lasting, as one thought inevitably leads to another. To elevate the physical world of the chessboard leads to seeing, and the necessity to think about, higher things. The sword meditates and concentrates, the cup contains emotional essence, the wand controls creative energies and the pentacle manifests in the world.

Divination Meanings

Initiation through the intellect. Lucidity and penetration. Aspiring to serve the world. Flexibility and juggling.

Reversed Meanings

Appearances hide reality, leading to seduction by power. Inflexibility.

I   MAGICIAN

♊ ♍ GEMINI   **MERCURY**   VIRGO ♍

HIGH PRIESTESS

Number II
The Moon
Gimel is wisdom

The Traditional High Priestess

The High Priestess in early tarot decks is called The Papess after the mythical Pope Joan of the ninth century, and is understood to be Juno, Diana, the priestess of the Eleusinian mysteries or the Celtic Triple Goddess. She is shown in the vestments of Isis, a crown of two horn-shaped crescents astride a lunar orb, a solar cross on her breast, her feet on a waxing crescent moon, and bearing a partially visible scroll. In some versions, the scroll is the TORA book of Hebrew law, and in others the words TORA are inscribed around a circle so that when read backwards they spell TAROT. She also bears the crossed silver and gold keys of St Peter, which signify papal authority. Her throne sits between black and white lotus pillars indicating the undeveloped powers of virginity. She carries a lotus flower, a lightning bolt, and is often accompanied by two camels, as the Hebrew letter *gimel* means camel.

The Symbolism of the High Priestess

The colour motif of the card is indigo and silver symbolic of the Moon; the horns and orb of Isis, the arch of the lunar cycle, the white and black pillars, the lotus, the crab and the camels are all common lunar symbols. Her rainbow-coloured robes are set off against the darkness of night; wisdom and power derive from understanding the polarities of day and night. The nature of the High Priestess is open, receptive, dark and changeable, although her possession of the TORA scrolls shows that the way to understanding is through unconscious processes. The camels walking in opposite directions, the keys of different metals and the crab, characterized by its sideways movement, all symbolize the unpredictable and contrary ways to the soul.

Divination Meanings

The High Priestess is the potential uniting intelligence of subconscious memory. Enlightenment brought to unconsciousness. The truth is hidden and may be discovered only through intuition, divination, feminine wisdom or revelation. Emotional matters. Foresight. Increase and fluctuation. Forces of nature. Artistic and psychic abilities.

Reversed Meanings

Secrecy. Emotional instability or enslavement. Decrease. Unused potential. Something hidden.

EMPRESS

Number III
The planet Venus
Daleth is life

The Traditional Empress

The Empress is seated on a throne with high wings, denoting a heavenly lineage, holding a cross-topped sceptre of physical power in her left hand. She carries a shield bearing a regal eagle of rebirth, symbolic of the earth mysteries, and her crowned head is surrounded by 12 stars, showing that she produces all souls. She is also the powerful Great Goddess or Earth Mother who has domain over Nature, especially the grain in the fields and the fruits of plants. She is the wilderness of the instincts, which must be subdued in order to be fruitful.

The Symbolism of the Empress

The Empress is the planet Venus, showing essential fecundity, the ability to embrace and love all fruits of the natural world and to bear the joys and sorrows of life and death. Her red throne of purest instinct is covered by the eyes of the all-seeing wisdom encoded in Life, and it sits on the surface of the sea surrounded by fields of grain, showing how her power emerges from the unconscious. The cypress tree grows naturally from the water, stressing the necessity for contact with the deep emotional core; the harvested sheaf of grain and her upturned lunar crescent show that leaving the womb of the Empress is a sacrifice which is required in order to dominate the baser instincts of life during the spiritual quest.

Divination Meanings

Following the path of harmony through conflict. Fruitfulness and fertility lead to attachment to earthy, physical values and the evolution of wealth and property. It corresponds to woman, mother, sister, wife, daughter and the nurturing and destructive sides of the feminine principle.

Reversed Meanings

Being dominated by materialism, overemotionality and possessiveness, leading to losses and infertility.

III

EMPRESS

♎ 8 TAURUS
LIBRA

VENUS

PISCES ♓

EMPEROR
Number IV
The sign Aries
Heh is speech

The Traditional Emperor

A regal man sits enthroned upon a cubic stone symbolizing power over the physical world of the instincts. His crossed legs and arms holding a sceptre and an orb show the first stage of integration of female and male, unconscious and conscious spiritual energies. He leans upon a semicircular crescent armrest and carries a shield displaying a royal eagle of authority and imperial soul, showing that he is paired with, but follows his Empress, as the masculine principle emerges from the feminine. He is accompanied by rams which signify virility and assertiveness.

The Symbolism of the Emperor

Aries is the fire sign, manifestating self-assertion, authority, and power over the instincts. The cubic throne has emerged from the unconsciousness of the sea on to the stability of the land, symbolizing the necessary ascendancy of the spiritual over the material. The root of his power is in the feminine unconscious, which has been controlled, and in his ability to utilize both feminine and masculine qualities. The surrounding countryside is aggressively martial, as the landscape of consciousness is harsh and unforgiving. The elevated checkerboard refers to the position of the King as a spiritual warrior – truth ultimately triumphs over physical power.

Divination Meanings

Lucid engagement with daily responsibilities creates increased perception and unity through effort. Self-assertion and expression. Great confidence and creativity result when the intellect triumphs over emotion. It is best to follow the path of one's own personality and its messages for success.

Reversed Meanings

One should guard against pride and selfishness. Exaggerated attraction to power and authority make for a barren person. Immaturity and weakness of character. Opposite qualities are Justice and Libra as balance, which suggest correct choices and equilibrium.

HIGH PRIEST

Number V
The sign Taurus
Vau is thought

The Traditional High Priest

Also called the Hierophant or the Pope, an old bearded man is seated between two pillars blessing two figures kneeling before him. His right hand is half-shut, concealing mysteries within his domain, and his left holds a triple-crossed staff which symbolizes ascent through the physical, emotional and spiritual realms. The figures before him parallel the keys inherited as symbols of his access both to the mundane world and kingdom of heaven.

The Symbolism of the High Priest

Taurus is the physical foundation from which the spiritual quest arises. A cubic throne, resting upon an endless chessboard, between lotus pillars supporting the vault of the heavens shows the duality of the world and the relationship between desire and liberation. The staff bisected by an orb of spirit bridges the gap between above and below, and is entwined by a serpent, implying that the mystery of time is within the understanding of the High Priest. The silver lunar and gold solar keys to the unconscious and conscious mind are overgrown by roses, which are vortexes of spiritual energy and symbolic of human redemption.

Divination Meanings

An opportunity to transform material desire into loving generosity. Ceremonial traditions bring guidance about worldly affairs. Overcoming physical needs produces freedom from a compulsive attachment. Artistic sensibility helps practical matters.

Reversed Meanings

Being possessed by the demands of mind and body. Unauthentic guidance caused by pedantry. Unorthodox and illegal acts are thoughtless. The opposite qualities are Death and Scorpio, which bode trials and testing to attain freedom.

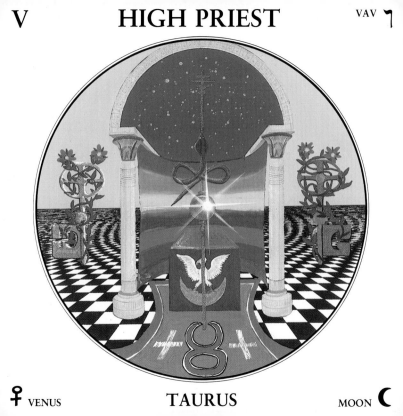

♀ VENUS   **TAURUS**   MOON ☾

LOVERS

Number VI
The sign Gemini
Zain is movement

The Traditional Lovers

A young man at a crossroads stands between a temptress on the right and a pure virgin on the left, indicating a choice. Within a solar disc is a winged cherub pointing an arrow at the figure on the right, implying a choice of experience over naivete. The marriage of male and female is an essential stage in the process of integration because the feminine leads the hero to discover his individuality and wholeness.

The Symbolism of the Lovers

Mercury is the choice of creative self-expression and duality between oneself and others, and of the mind, as mediator between the physical and emotional bodies. The central Mars figure is a divine intermediary, desiring change, which must make relationship (with flanking Venus) whichever direction it turns – each Mercurial choice involves a parting, if only from one level to another. Twelve flaming apples indicate temptations of desire. Duality between personality and soul is only resolved by the higher self, as a Sagittarian archer within the spiritual Sun, creating an apex for the triangle and a way for resolution.

Divination Meanings

It is advisable to go to an impartial third party or a higher aspect of oneself in order to resolve inner or outer disputes. Problems caused by crystallization and rigidity. Accept and value the process more than the outcome. A choice with more significance than outer appearances suggest. An opportunity to establish control of the soul through higher awareness.

Reversed Meanings

Infatuation with appearances and devotion to choices of direction is an avoidance of choosing a higher goal. Vacillating between opposites diffuses effort. Opposite values are Temperance and Sagittarius which counsel a philosophical attitude and one-pointedness.

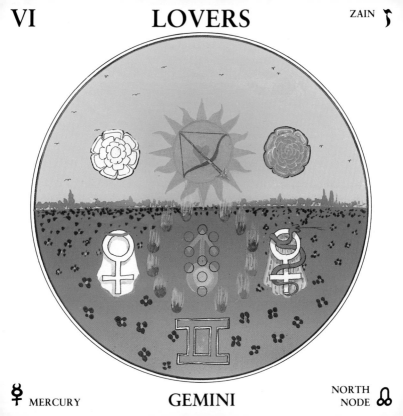

CHARIOT

Number VII
The sign Cancer
Cheth is sight

The Traditional Chariot

A young prince (mind) rides a canopied chariot (body) drawn by two horses or sphinxes (emotions) with exaggerated female bodies, which are facing opposite directions. Epaulettes made of crescent moons with human faces adorn his uniform, showing dual feelings and the contradiction between inner desire and outer expression. The starry canopy shows his association with the spiritual and the realm of higher emotional balance.

The Symbolism of the Chariot

Cancer is the home of the soul, ruled by the Moon as the habit-forming emotional attachment to home and family. Exalted by Jupiter, a hero returns to his castellated home, sensitive about whether to accept its security or maintain his freedom to respond to outer influences from the world. The chariot is symbolic of the body drawn by conflicting emotions, aroused by the feminine, and expresses the necessity to conquer them. The phallic lingum on the shield portrays the sexual dominance of desire, and the sphinxes the potential positive and negative feelings which result. The city walled by human bones shows that past patterns are deadly and result in stagnation and crystallization.

Divination Meanings

Controlling mind triumphs over obstacles by harnessing emotions and applying a higher world view. Resolution of inner conflict. Expansion due to nurturing others or through women. Sensitivity transmuted into service. Property acquisitions.

Reversed Meanings

Being overly attached to freedom is in itself a restriction. Quarrels. The inability to control conflicting feelings which leads to depression and coldness. Division between physical and emotional realities. The opposite quality is the Devil and Capricorn as bondage to materialism.

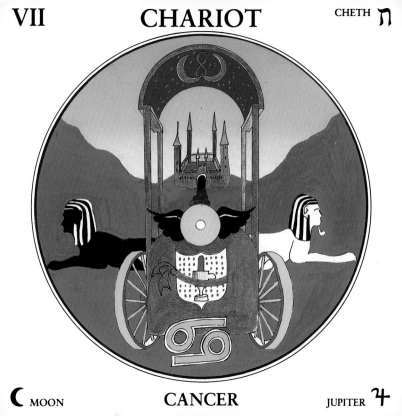

STRENGTH

Number VIII
The sign Leo
Teth is hearing

The Traditional Strength

A beautiful woman is the unconscious opening the mouth of a lion, showing her easy control over the apparent dominance of consciousnes. Around his neck is a chain of flowers symbolizing his need for awareness of surrounding souls in order to break free from the bond of his self-centredness. Her hat is shaped like a lemniscate, symbolizing infinity, showing her relationship to the Magician in taming the Self. The lunar virgin of discrimination does not fear dangerous encounters with instinctive desires; by exercising love and softness she prevails.

The Symbolism of Strength

Leo is the power and fortitude of self-consciousness in overcoming the wilful personality, ruled by the Sun, the spiritual self which resides within the centre of the psyche. With her seven arrows of organization and directed manifestation, Diana the virgin huntress dominates destructive desire, symbolized by the lion. Overcoming passion is a source of great inner strength, and confronting fear of the self produces mastery. When the heart is pure, even the great beasts may be tamed.

Divination Meanings

The courage to look within gives the power to conquer the natural world, no matter how omnipotent it appears. Mind dominates matter through the self. Ruling the self is the achievement of rulership.

Reversed Meanings

Abusing and taking advantage of selfish power. Self-centredness is the most glamorous weakness. The opposite quality is embodied in the Stars and Aquarius as the dissolution of individuality in brotherhood.

VIII   STRENGTH TETH ט

SUN   **LEO**   PLUTO ♇

HERMIT

Number IX
The sign Virgo
Yod is work

The Traditional Hermit

An ancient wise man, almost totally hidden by his hooded cloak, starts out on a journey across a vast valley of life experiences. His lantern hides the light of God and he supports his weight with a spiritual staff. A serpent writhes on the barren ground at his feet.

The Symbolism of the Hermit

Mercury fertilizes itself and transforms simplicity into understanding by releasing conflicting pictures to achieve harmony through the application of perceptive mind. The staff is divided into sections, representing the seven sacred centres and the seven planets in the heavens, and it bridges the space between the barren and fruitful trees, between which also hang the rainbow veil of illusory pictures of the world. The cloak obscures the Hermit's true esoteric identity until his quest has reached its conclusion on top of the distant mountain at the ordained time. The search is lonely, but the way is enlightened by the lantern of faith emblazoned with the Seal of Solomon, the symbol of integration of downward emotional and physical impulses and upward intellectual and spiritual aspirations.

Divination Meanings

The emphasis on hidden meanings must be overcome patiently with introspection and meditation. Through renunciation and service wisdom may be attained. Lonely travel towards a distant goal. Withdrawal from the world is beneficial.

Reversed Meanings

Concealment and disguise mask true intentions. Unreasonable caution and fear of exposure. Obsession with physical perfection. The opposite quality is the Moon and Pisces indicating sacrifice.

☿ MERCURY   **VIRGO**   MERCURY ☿

WHEEL OF FORTUNE

Number X
The planet Jupiter
Kaph is grace

The Traditional Wheel of Fortune

Upon a small boat is a vertical wheel with six spokes spinning three animals: a sword-wielding sphinx is on top, a jackal is ascending on the right, a snake is descending on the left. The four animals of the apocalypse are included on the wheel, which is turned by a pair of intertwined snakes.

The Symbolism of the Wheel of Fortune

Jupiter transcends time, ruling the higher mind of Sagittarius and the devotion of Pisces. The image evokes the eastern wheel of birth, death and rebirth to which all souls are bound, as all souls originate in the unconscious sea. After the withdrawal of the Hermit, the initiate must recognize that experiences originate from within. The only freedom from the eternal circularity of the periphery is within the centre – the animals moving up or down on the wheel perpetually change position. Only the sphinx is above the entire process, having entered its spiritual position via the centre. The wheel upon which he is bound is the world view of the initiate.

Divination Meanings

Mastery over destiny requires a higher understanding of the process. A desire for adventure, escape and worldly success. Understanding the laws of karma and adopting a larger world view.

Reversed Meanings

An old-fashioned attitude which needs to be changed. Unexpected bad luck caused by not trusting the process. Unpredictable outer influences which adversely affect events.

JUSTICE

The Traditional Justice

A crowned woman, seated on a throne between two pillars, holds an upward-pointing sword and scales. The image is reminiscent of the Egyptian judgement with Osiris weighing the soul, and the sword symbolizes divine retribution.

The Symbolism of Justice

Venus rules the process of coming to a decision based on consideration of two relative points of view, which represent soul and personality. Saturn exalted shows that both partners are either defined or limited by their relationship. The sword signifies the primary components of a balanced mind: lawfulness and awareness. The threefold nature of the suspended pans and the relationship of both pans to the figure of Justice shows the necessity for a higher spiritual position as a resolution to all relationships. Mental awareness must expand and integrate with reality in order that the imbalances in life are righted.

Divination Meanings

Deliberation leads to the recognition that the cause of all imbalance is within, and that the ability to restore balance is also within. Harmony, equality, karmic balance and sublimation. Using influence in political and personal spheres.

Reversed Meanings

Indecision or acting without deliberation. Lacking balance. Blaming others for one's own lack of equilibrium. The opposite quality is the Emperor and Aries where self-assurance is paramount.

XII HANGED MAN MEM נ

♓ PISCES   **WATER** NEPTUNE   CANCER· ♋

DEATH

Number XIII
The sign Scorpio
Nun is smell

The Traditional Death

A skeleton scythes severed human heads, hands and feet. One of the heads resting on the ground wears a crown. Plants sprout up from the ground on which the limbs rest.

The Symbolism of Death

Scorpio has domain over the process of testing, separation, death and putrefaction. Its rulers are Mars indicating change, breakdown and fighting spirit, and Pluto the transformer, bringer of war and large-scale change. The grim reaper has power over all beings, regardless of rank, beauty or wealth, but is also the guardian of the underworld of the unconscious, out of which all life and matter comes. Limbs are sown in the ground, showing that death is a form of rebirth, a cleansing required for the seed of new existence. The triangular process of growth, maturity and decay governs all life, within which the lotus of wholeness grows out of a skull sitting upon a turtle, symbolic of the resurrection of the soul. The rainbow bridge expresses the upward transformation accompanying the triumph of aspiration as it connects the higher Self and the personality, which must die and transform before integration.

Divination Meanings

Loss leading to renewal. The necessity for existing situations to end before a higher resolution may result. Breakdown as a necessary precondition for rebirth. Transformers. Letting go of possessions, ideas or justifications. Outer change is necessary to prevent physical illness.

Reversed Meanings

Stagnation and resistance to change. Being victimized by worldly forces. Being attracted to dangerous tests. The opposite quality is the High Priest and Taurus showing the need for grounding.

XIII

DEATH

NUN נ

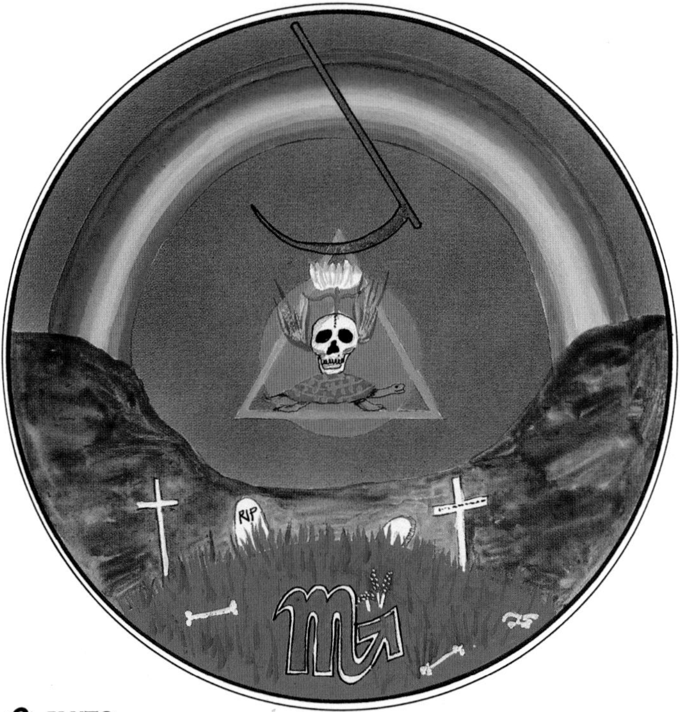

♂ ♇ PLUTO
MARS

SCORPIO

URANUS ♅

TEMPERANCE

Number XIV
The sign Sagittarius
Samekh is sleep

The Traditional Temperance

A winged angel from Heaven pours a mercurial fluid from a gold vase into a silver vase. Above her head is a ring of stars, showing high aspiration. She stands with one foot in the water and the other on land, upon which grows single plants. In the background are lush hills.

The Symbolism of Temperance

Sagittarius indicates the necessity for high mindedness and religious contemplation, acting through its ruling planet Jupiter, the planet of moral aspiration and transcendence. The spiralling snake of time enwraps the winged Venusian love symbol showing the eternal nature of true love. The transforming Aquarian fluid poured between vessels represents the fertilizing energy passing from male to female. The soul only temporarily takes the form of a womblike vessel within which the uterine fluid is the medium for the new being, on its journey between lifetimes. Persephone bridged life and death by nourishing souls in the underworld preceding their return to life.

Divination Meanings

The seed of future events has been sown, but the outcome requires patience. Self-control and accommodation are necessary for proper integration of influences which initially do not fit together. Temporary stalemate followed by reconciliation. Nothing lost, nothing gained.

Reversed Meanings

Impatience and conflict of interests. Lack of success caused by the inability to relate to others.

4 JUPITER   SAGITTARIUS   SOUTH ℧ NODE

DEVIL

Number XV
The sign Capricorn
Ayin is anger

The Traditional Devil

A hideous figure with batwings, goat's legs and talons instead of feet squats upon a dark, earthbound pedestal to which two piteous animalistic human figures with horns are chained, showing the danger of excessive attachment to passion and materialism. The Devil holds an extinguished phallic torch in his left hand, making all dark, and his right hand is raised, symbolizing the dominance of instincts and the elevation of chaos over order. The figure is hermaphroditic, possessing both breasts and penis, part cloven-hoofed animal and part winged bird or bat – it is a composite of the lower qualities of humanity. The atmosphere of the card is dank and evokes the underworld.

The Symbolism of the Devil

Capricorn shows the dominance of worldly power and the difficulties of withstanding temptation. The ruling Saturn is embossed on the wings as the conflict between egocentricity and self-restraint, while Mars exalted is the necessity to resist ambition turning to arrogance. The Devil as the god Pan is temptation and attachment to the delights of the material world of the senses, but the weak chains show the potential to overcome self-inflicted bondage. The distorted magic circle symbolizes the entrapment of humanity within the wheel of time and its pleasures. The inverted pentangle head is human nature descending into the underworld. The Devil's function is as guardian of the threshold whom the initiate must pass.

Divination Meanings

The necessity to overcome self-centred temptations of the physical world of the senses. Loss of power and money. The end of an affair due to intrigue or sexual pressure. Excessive materialism prevents growth. Arrogance, stagnation, unforeseen difficulties caused by oneself.

Reversed Meanings

Overcoming reliance on the material world, the beginning of understanding and directed willpower. The opposite quality is symbolized by the Chariot and Cancer as sensitivity to the unconscious.

TOWER

Number XVI
The planet Mars
Peh is riches

The Traditional Tower

An ominous tower, sometimes called the House of God, is shattered by a lightning-bolt, splitting off its top and throwing out male and female figures headlong. In the lower part of the tower are two openings with a third higher up, showing the resolution of lower physical and emotional instincts in the spiritual impulse.

The Symbolism of the Tower

Mars shows that keeping tension inside leads to forced changes in one's condition as the urge to change the world starts with oneself. Scorpionic strength is created through unavoidable difficulties. The incarnating soul is thrown into the world of duality headfirst by a thunderbolt which represents both fate and, in a Buddhist sense, high spiritual direction. Dependency on the outer world often prevents true spiritual development, until radical changes ensue once these values are questioned. The top of the phallic tower is sheared off and the male and female falling figures show that the desire to keep issues of duality within leads to separation and breakdown. Past patterns are shattered and the future requires rebuilding, but the original trial was sent by God. The streaming yods (eyes) are the archetypal world of the divine as 22 ways of seeing the next stage of the quest.

Divination Meanings

Total change and loss of security leading to a new beginning. Unexpected disruptions caused by being overprotective. Unwillingness to look at unrest inside. Loss of stability leading to a breakthrough. Reversals of fortune.

Reversed Meanings

Continuing repression. Self-induced difficulties. Financial or property losses. Rebirth at the cost of extreme difficulty. The opposite is the Empress and Venus as consolidation and integration.

XVI TOWER PEH

SCORPIO
ARIES MARS CAPRICORN

STARS

Number XVII
The sign Aquarius
Tzaddi is taste

The Traditional Stars

A loving and devoted woman kneels with one knee on the fertile ground and the other in an unrushing stream, showing how Venus unites earth and sea. From the two vases she holds, water is poured from one on to the land and from the other into the stream. Above her head is a halo of seven stars, with one larger than the rest. Near her on the fertile landscape is a pure white flower above which a butterfly of the soul flutters.

The Symbolism of the Stars

Aquarius bears two streams of water, representing ideas which contain the seed of opposition within themselves, ruled by Uranus as the progressive spiritual inspiration from above and Saturn as the necessary grounding of idealism. The Queen of Heaven is shown as a Venusian pyramid with a crystal apex, crowned by the stars of the Great Bear, the seven governing spirits of our universe, with Sirius as their cosmic guide. Golden and silver vases pour the essence of male and female back on to the earth, their receptacle and home. The butterfly of psyche gathers the nectar of experience to be distilled into honey from the pure white lily, the flower of consciousness. The sacred red ibis (Thoth) is magical understanding emerging from the unconscious which guides the process of the soul's initiation. The falcon of Horus and the eagle of Zeus bracket the stars which are the source of their transcendent light and luminous space.

Divination Meanings

Lifeless areas of life may be fertilized by looking beyond immediate attractions to discover the depths. With faith and hope, plans for the future will come to fruition. Astrological influences combined with human understanding lead to deeper and more fertile relationships.

Reversed Meanings

Impatience for results inhibits positive relationships. Eccentric and ambitious plans without a solid foundation lead to disappoinment and pessimism. Exaggerated indolence and weakness. The opposite is Fortitude and Leo as one-pointedness and consciousness of the present.

URANUS
SATURN

AQUARIUS

MOON

Number XVIII
The sign Pisces
Qoph is mirth

The Traditional Moon

A wolf and a dog, representing animalistic instincts demanding expression, howl at the moon's face looming large in a night sky. They have come from and protect the two flanking towers, the rigid structures of their masters. A large red lobster, as the higher self, emerges on to the land from a still pool of past memories into which 22 yods fall as tears. Two winding paths, which come from beside the pool, join and curve away into the distance towards the horizon.

The Symbolism of the Moon

Pisces is the receptive, psychic and mystical openness of those having direct contact within, ruled by Neptune indicating a sensitivity to moral choices, signified by the black jackal and white dog within white and black pyramids, edifices of prejudice and convention. Positive feelings lie at the core of what appears to be negative, and vice versa. The Moon counsels balancing feeling against past experiences. Jupiter ruling is meditation upon the hidden forces of nature. Venus is exalted in Pisces showing the integration of positive and negative forces through love which the path requires. The Moon goddess Selene is positive instinct beyond systems and concepts. Souls return to the Moon after death, but are within her domain during life as well, and abide by her laws of darkness.

Divination Meanings

Obstacles from the past apparently preventing progress must be negotiated and balanced, until they decline and eventually disappear. Meditation can compensate for entrapment by outer influences beyond one's control. Danger from outside. An intense and emotional love life.

Reversed Meanings

Psychic life is adversely influenced by dreams or drugs. Destructive impulses must be understood and rejected. Dissatisfaction and failure caused by deception or hidden enemies. The opposite qualities are the Hermit and Virgo; the avoidance of emotional involvement.

XVIII   MOON   QOPH

NEPTUNE
JUPITER   PISCES   VENUS

SUN

Number XIX
The Sun
Resh is fertility

The Traditional Sun

A pair of naked children with nothing to hide clasp hands and join together within a walled garden, a structure protecting them from outside influences. From above the sun shines its spirituality as golden rays.

The Symbolism of the Sun

The Sun is our central source of light, creativity and spiritual happiness, and rules the sign Leo, where formative energy expresses the true self, and exalts Aries, where consciousness of the divine plan is made manifest in the individual. The stronger the lower material structures of an individual or society, the more essential it is for the higher spiritual rays to penetrate. Sunflowers follow the sun's movement across the sky as the spiritual path must be followed for life to be full. The Gemini symbol is squared in the circle of the integration of opposites, and is itself within a circular wreath of the yearly process of nature governed and fuelled by the sun. Love and friendship bring contact with the warmth and creativity of the sun.

Divination Meanings

The awakened spirit of friendship and brotherhood is freedom from confinement in obsolete structures. Marriage is the merging with another being. The ability to experience life and to attract others to higher ideals and actions. Inner light and inner worth.

Reversed Meanings

Egocentric and isolated belief systems prevent relationshps from flowering and growing. Barricading oneself inside is detrimental to health. Ruthlessness and the lust for power leads to a lack of support from above. The opposite quality is the World and Saturn as restriction and seriousness in existence.

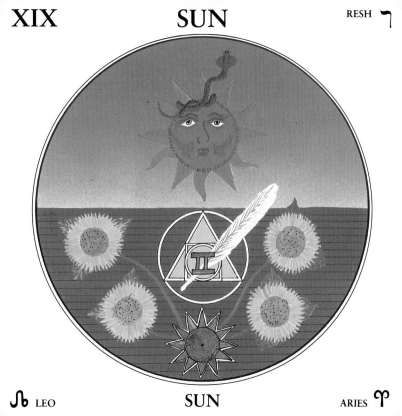

JUDGEMENT

Number XX
The element Fire and the planet Pluto
Shin is vices

The Traditional Judgement

A winged angel within the clouds blows a trumpet of atonement, decorated with a cross-emblazoned banner, to people of all ages emerging from coffins and graves.

The Symbolism of the Judgement

The element Fire shows the energy of heaven which shatters structures to unite humanity, and Pluto which shows the required destruction of existing forms before regeneration occurs. Death and destruction are only preludes to rebirth in a new and higher state, as all causes must be transcended. The coffin is life's structure, within which humanity is trapped, floating on the surface of the unconscious – yet male and female differences must be integrated to form the central child, which is unity. The whole scene is presided over by the winged solar disc of the law of the cosmos.

Divination Meanings

Success despite difficulties which force an about turn. The decision to complete an action leads to the termination of current partnerships. Accomplishing the work of transformation. Changes of position and beliefs.

Reversed Meanings

Being required to make decisions which shatter existing relationships. Delay, transient glory and then success.

XX   JUDGEMENT   SHIN ש

SCORPIO   FIRE PLUTO   LEO

WORLD

Number XXI
The planet Saturn
Tau is peace

The Traditional World

Also called the Universe, a veiled young woman with crossed legs stands within an elliptical laurel and rose wreath, holding a wand in each hand. At the four corners are the symbolic figures of the fixed zodiacal signs: the bull of Taurus, the lion of Leo, the eagle of Scorpio and the man of Aquarius.

The Symbolism of the World

Saturn is physical form and existence as governed by the mechanism of time, portrayed as a spherical alchemical vessel in space. Capricorn is the limitation of laws made physically manifest, and Aquarius is the same laws which control and describe the divine plan to which humanity is subject. The exaltation in Libra is the integration of opposites on the battleground of the self in its experience of life, evoking genetic molecules and planetary movements around the sun. The World is the completion of the tarot sequence, the absolute and definitive marker. The spiritual process originates in the heavens, and its four markers are astrological, astronomical and cosmic cornerstones. The World is the father of form, the originator and definer of life, as he is simultaneously the grim reaper and taker of life in death, both processes integral to the work of time. The maternal aspect of the World is the Great Mother, out of whom all existence ensues, who wields her laws through the immeasurable cosmos.

Divination Meanings

Success ensues by meeting and abiding by spiritual and physical laws. Completing the cosmic sequence and understanding the world as it is. Trusting fate is a requirement for synthesis. Hard work and obedience lead to eventual satisfaction and success.

Reversed Meanings

A lack of understanding of cosmic laws leads to failure in all ways. Faulty vision needs meditation. The opposite quality is the Sun as pointedness and a sense of individual self.

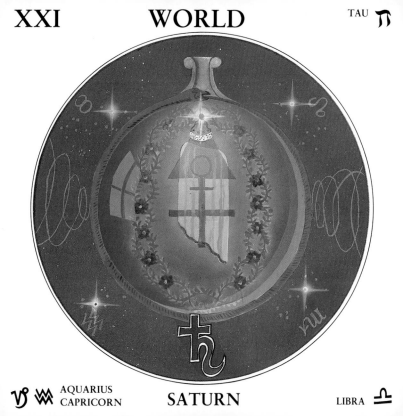

WAND QUEEN — ARIES THRONE
PENTACLE QUEEN — CAPRICORN THRONE
SWORD QUEEN — LIBRA THRONE
CUP QUEEN — CANCER THRONE

WAND KING — LEO CROWN
PENTACLE KING — TAURUS CROWN
SWORD KING — AQUARIUS CROWN
CUP KING — SCORPIO CROWN

WAND PRINCE — SAGITTARIUS CHARIOT
PENTACLE PRINCE — VIRGO CHARIOT
SWORD PRINCE — GEMINI CHARIOT
CUP PRINCE — PISCES CHARIOT

WAND PRINCESS — FIRE PALACE
PENTACLE PRINCESS — EARTH PALACE
SWORD PRINCESS — AIR PALACE
CUP PRINCESS — WATER PALACE

Chapter 3

THE COURT CARDS

The court cards are considered primarily as personifications, characters of the tarot drama, and intermediaries between the major arcana and the numbered cards. For example, the Sword court cards could be described as follows: the Sword King as a mature man with dark hair and eyes; the Sword Queen as a stern and sad brown-haired and brown-eyed young woman; while the Sword Princess as a brown-eyed and brown-haired girl. The Cup court cards are fair, the wands are blondes with blue or hazel eyes, and the pentacles are swarthy, black-eyed, black-haired and stocky. Each court card describes a specific person.

The introduction of astrological correspondences brings an even greater degree of identification to the court cards, because each court card corresponds to a particular sign of the zodiac, and possesses not only the equivalent physical appearance but personality qualities as well. The Wand Queen is not only a blonde with blue eyes but is an Aries as well, making her self assertive and dynamic. The advantage of sign meanings is that it is also possible to identify the qualities of the people described by court cards. The person indicated may not necessarily be a woman, but it will be someone with Aries behaviour and appearance.

The four Queens are elemental Thrones representing the cardinal signs, which initiate action and are considered the most powerful and dynamic of astrological signs: Aries, Cancer, Libra and Capricorn. They are leaders and provoke behaviour fitting their element, so the Sword Queen is a Libran match-maker, diplomat or sexual politician.

The four Kings are Crowns representing the fixed signs Taurus, Leo, Scorpio and Aquarius, also shown in the card of the World or the Universe. These signs sustain, manifest and hold powerfully to their elemental qualities. They do not alter their position easily, and tend to be very stubborn and stable. For example, the Pentacle King is a Taurean with feet firmly planted on the ground, secure in the material world and wanting to stay that way.

The four Princes are Chariots showing the mobility of the mutable signs Gemini, Virgo, Sagittarius and Pisces, three of which are 'double' signs with more than a little duality and changeability, and which continually alter their position. When the Cup Prince is reversed you could expect to meet a charming Piscean who will make you feel like his true and only love, but will forget you in five minutes.

The four Princesses live within Palaces representing the pure elements and are less specific than their elders. The Wand Princess is a person with an abundance of energy but lacks a direction in which to apply it.

The 16 court cards have colour-coded backgrounds which link them to a sign of the zodiac; they rule certain times of the year as well.

THE WAND SUIT

The element Fire
Aries, Leo and Sagittarius

The fire signs initiate each of the three octaves of the horoscope and provide the energy and assertiveness which fuels the zodiac. Essentially the fire signs are expressions of pure spirit manifesting as strong will, aspiration, inspiration, action, courage and daring, rashness and aggression. They are hot, active, masculine, individual, unemotional, dynamic, unstable, extrovert, intuitive. Qualities they produce are creativity, drama, intensity, progress, change, evolution. Feelings they engender are joy, anger, enthusiasm.

THE PENTACLE SUIT

The element Earth
Taurus, Virgo and Capricorn

The earth signs are the manifestation into physical form of the energy generated by the spirit and create, stabilize and sustain the physical bodies. Essentially the earth signs are physical: practical, material, conservative, possessive, secure, industrious and thrifty. They are cold, passive, feminine, individual, emotional, static, stable, introvert and sensitive. Qualities they express are common sense, structure, resistance to change, tangibility, emotional reliability. Shadow qualities of earth signs are pig-headedness, intransigence, excessive passivity, overly practical, unfeeling, distant, materialistic obsessions and a general resistance to movement and change.

THE SWORD SUIT

The element Air
Gemini, Libra and Aquarius

The air signs are unstable, wilful and self-expressive and make relationships possible. They are expressions of pure mind manifesting as strong ideas, perception, alertness, versatility, observation, cooperation, compatibility and nervousness. They are cold, active, masculine, related, unemotional, dynamic, unstable, extrovert, thinking and detached. Qualities they express are humane, detached, dualistic, vacillating, alert, logical, quickness in mind and body. Shadow qualities of air signs are their abstraction and distance, lack of intimacy, intellectual criticism, ambiguity and lack of constancy.

THE CUP SUIT

The element Water
Cancer, Scorpio and Pisces

The water signs are the most difficult to define, being subjective, personal and receptive to outer influences. Essentially the water signs are value systems or feelings which are often unexpressed or expressed as emotional, sensitive, mediumistic, impressionable, imaginative, psychic, secretive and visionary. They are cold, passive, feminine, dependent, emotional, change-able, unstable, introvert and feeling. Qualities they generate are romantic, indulgent, expressive, valued, imaginative, devotional and erotic. Shadow qualities are two-sided, scatty, overemotional, obsessive, hypochondriac, psychosomatic and overly influenced by others.

THE WAND COURT CARDS

WAND QUEEN

Throne of Fire – Aries   (21 March to 21 Apr)
Initiating energy and the power of self-assertion. Aries is fiery, masculine, cardinal, dry, hot, vernal, eastern, single-bodied, animalistic, irrational and dominant.

Divination Meanings: Persistent energy, commanding pride and passionate stubbornness.

Reversed Meanings: Vanity, snobbery, obstinately tyrannical or jealous.

WAND KING

Crown of Fire – Leo   (23 July to 22 Aug)
Fixed energy manifested in constant self-consciousness, dominance of the self and great expansiveness. Leo is fiery, masculine, fixed, dry, hot, summery, southern, single-bodied, animalistic, irrational and dominant.

Divination Meanings: Impulsive. Strength and fortitude. Nobility and courage, but easily deceived.

Reversed Meanings: Autocratic, arrogant and self-centred. Unethical boasting.

WAND PRINCE

Chariot of Fire – Sagittarius   (23 Nov to 21 Dec)
Changing energy and an expansive world view. Sagittarius is fiery, masculine, mutable, damp, hot, wintry, northern, half-animal and half-human, irrational and changeable.

Divination Meanings: A messenger. Impetuousness. Swift thoughts and actions. Foreign philosophies and attitudes. Generosity.

Reversed Meanings: Abandonment. Flight or departure from reason. Separation and discord.

WAND PRINCESS

Palace of Fire – Spirit
Pure intuition and energy before manifestation.

Divination Meanings: Brilliant and daring energies. Pure aspiration. Acting upon instinct. Adolescent enthusiasm.

Reversed Meanings: Easily perturbed. Superficial and incorrect intuitions. A betrayal of trust. Lacking energy.

WAND QUEEN

ARIES   THRONE

WAND KING

LEO   CROWN

WAND PRINCE

SAGITTARIUS   CHARIOT

WAND PRINCESS

FIRE   PALACE

THE PENTACLE COURT CARDS

PENTACLE QUEEN

Throne of Earth – Capricorn   (22 Dec to 19 Jan)
Initiating sensation as a prelude to control over the physical environment. Capricorn is earthy, feminine, cardinal, dry, cold, wintry, southern, single, animal, irrational and independent.

Divination Meanings: Great desire and ambition together with hard work lead to honour and wealth. Practical and sensible.

Reversed Meanings: Drudgery. Trapped by responsibilities. Materialism.

PENTACLE KING

Crown of Earth – Taurus   (21 Apr to 20 May)
Fixed sensation is practical and cautious, but is bound by the physical. Taurus is earthy, feminine, fixed, wet, warm, vernal, northern and eastern, singular, animal, rational and dependent.

Divination Meanings: Business concerns. A great capacity for endurance. Cautious and trustworthiness. Slow and steady wins the race.

Reversed Meanings: Unemotional dullness. Disinclined to understand. Avaricious. Furious with the world.

PENTACLE PRINCE

Chariot of Earth – Virgo   (23 Aug to 22 Sept)
Changeable sensation manifested as a preoccupation with the body, health and diet. Virgo is earthy, feminine, mutable, wet, warm, autumnal, northern and western, singular, humane, rational and dependent.

Divination Meanings: Perception, discrimination and perfectionalism leads to insularity. Preoccupied with occupational matters.

Reversed Meanings: Indolence and interference. Hypochondriac. Overly concerned with the physical. Picky. Easily misled.

PENTACLE PRINCESS

Palace of Earth – Body
Pure sensation without an object.

Divination Meanings: Honour and responsibility. Pure physical responses. Property which has presence. Issues of ownership.

Reversed Meanings: Overcautiousness. Hypercritical of oneself and others.

PENTACLE QUEEN

CAPRICORN   THRONE

PENTACLE KING

TAURUS   CROWN

PENTACLE PRINCE

VIRGO   CHARIOT

PENTACLE PRINCESS

EARTH   PALACE

THE SWORD COURT CARDS

SWORD QUEEN

Throne of Air – Libra   (23 Sep to 22 Oct)
The lawgiver, peacemaker, equilibrator in partnership with others and the world. Libra is airy, masculine, cardinal, dry, cold, autumnal, northern and western, two-sided, humane, rational and obeying.

Divination Meanings: Starting an association. Intuition and criticism. Creative surroundings. Emotions and affection.

Reversed Meanings: Ending an association. Excessive criticism.

SWORD KING

Crown of Air – Aquarius   (20 Jan to 18 Feb)
Fixed mind manifested in strong, unyielding ideas and attitudes. Aquarius is airy, masculine, fixed, dry, cold, wintry, southern and eastern, double bodied, humane, rational and obeying.

Divination Meanings: A decided opinion. Abstraction. Detachment. Intellectuality. Unchangeable attitudes. Groups of people with common long-range ideals.

Reversed Meanings: Unsettled mind. Incorrect opinions. Inflexibility. Acting without forethought. Unrealistic. Unreliable friends.

SWORD PRINCE

Chariot of Air – Gemini   (21 May to 20 Jun)
Changing mind imitates, and speaks and acts without reflection. Gemini is airy, masculine, mutable, dry, cold, vernal, northern and eastern, two-sided, humane, irrational and independent.

Divination Meanings: Activity. Cleverness. Skill. Verbal jousting. Fond of changes. Versatile. Lacking continuity. Persuasion. A short trip.

Reversed Meanings: Inactivity. Dullness. Superficial skills. Irresponsible words. Fixed. Being too easily persuaded. Irresolute. Uncertain.

SWORD PRINCESS

Palace of Air – Mind
Pure mind and ideas before manifestation.

Divination Meanings: Pure instinctive intellect. Mind without direction. A superficial grasp of matters.

Reversed Meanings: Spying. Faulty logic and judgement. Incorrect instincts.

SWORD QUEEN

LIBRA   THRONE

SWORD KING

AQUARIUS   CROWN

SWORD PRINCE

GEMINI   CHARIOT

SWORD PRINCESS

AIR   PALACE

THE CUP COURT CARDS

CUP QUEEN

Throne of Water – Cancer   (21 Jun to 22 Jul)
The origin of feelings which create sympathetic and emotional attitudes. Cancer is watery, feminine, cardinal, wet, warm, summery, northern, two-sided, inhuman, irrational and dependent.

Divination Meanings: Receptive and reflective feelings. Tranquillity. Kind nurturing. Family acceptance.

Reversed Meanings: Overly protective. Illusory and mediumistic leanings.

CUP KING

Crown of Water – Scorpio   (23 Oct to 22 Nov)
Fixed feelings which are powerful, deep and consuming. Scorpio is watery, feminine, fixed, wet, cold, autumnal, southern and western, singular, inhuman, irrational and independent.

Divination Meanings: A subtle reliance on others. Secret influences. Ruthlessness followed by remorse.

Reversed Meanings: Ruthless and merciless without conscience. Dishonesty leads to a loss of security. Manipulative. Disappointment.

CUP PRINCE

Chariot of Water – Pisces   (19 Feb to 20 Mar)
Changeable feelings lead to openness, sensitivity and responsiveness. Pisces is watery, feminine, mutable wet, cold, wintery, southern and eastern, two-sided, inhuman, irrational and dependent.

Divination Meanings: A passive and graceful response. Hidden feelings or devotion. Sensitive but superficial. Fateful and destined emotional attitudes.

Reversed Meanings: Breaking with destiny. Seduction through intoxication. Indolence. Idealism and devotion separates one from reality.

CUP PRINCESS

Palace of Water – Emotion
Pure feeling.

Divination Meanings: Grace and gentleness lead to romantic rapture, dreaming and idealism. Fantasies about reality.

Reversed Meanings: Being too susceptible to others' feelings. Depending on the environment. Changeable emotions.

CUP QUEEN

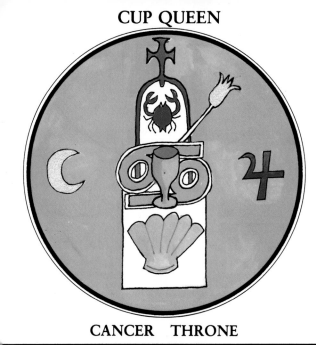

CANCER THRONE

CUP KING

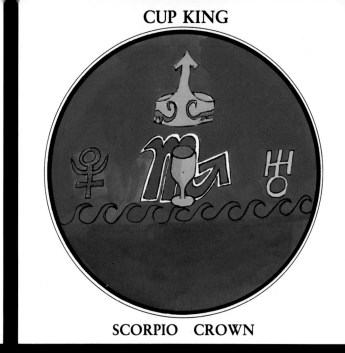

SCORPIO CROWN

CUP PRINCE

PISCES CHARIOT

CUP PRINCESS

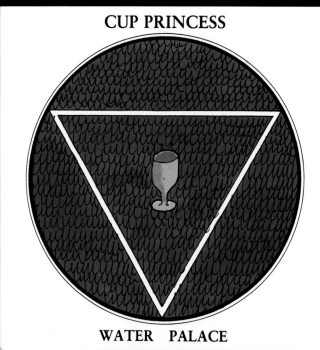

WATER PALACE

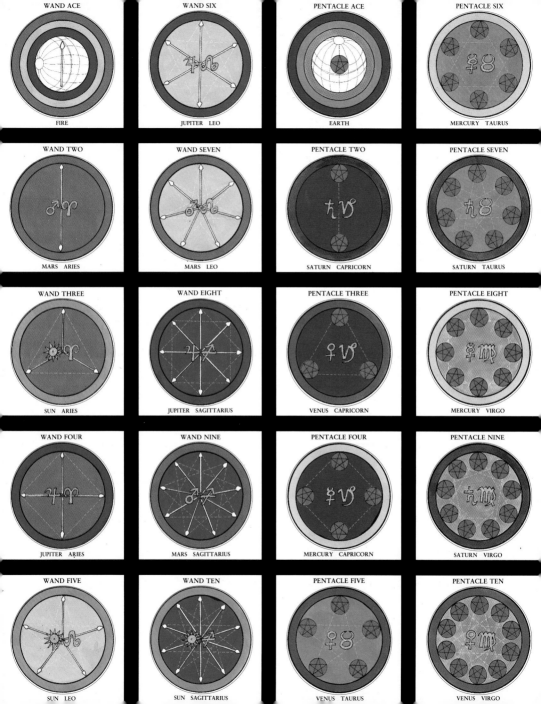

WAND ACE	WAND SIX	PENTACLE ACE	PENTACLE SIX
FIRE	JUPITER LEO	EARTH	MERCURY TAURUS

WAND TWO	WAND SEVEN	PENTACLE TWO	PENTACLE SEVEN
MARS ARIES	MARS LEO	SATURN CAPRICORN	SATURN TAURUS

WAND THREE	WAND EIGHT	PENTACLE THREE	PENTACLE EIGHT
SUN ARIES	JUPITER SAGITTARIUS	VENUS CAPRICORN	MERCURY VIRGO

WAND FOUR	WAND NINE	PENTACLE FOUR	PENTACLE NINE
JUPITER ARIES	MARS SAGITTARIUS	MERCURY CAPRICORN	SATURN VIRGO

WAND FIVE	WAND TEN	PENTACLE FIVE	PENTACLE TEN
SUN LEO	SUN SAGITTARIUS	VENUS TAURUS	VENUS VIRGO

Chapter 4

THE
MINOR
ARCANA

The minor arcana is the fabric of tarot, finer values which represent the decanates, the 10 degree divisions of the zodiac signs. The major arcana is the powerful archetype of signs, planets and elements, the court cards are personifications, and the minor arcana is a series of actions.

The minor arcana is composed of 10 cards (ace to 10) in each of the four tarot suits. In traditional tarot the 10 cards form a sequence of development through each suit, beginning with the ace as the essence or spirit of the element and ending with the 10 as the completion or culmination.

Historically, the sequence of 10 numbers has its origin in creation myths, forms the organizational core of most myths and fairy stories, and is the archetypal sequence of psychological states. In this way the numbers act simultaneously within the psyche and in the outside world, as cosmic linkages.

The Mandala Astrological Tarot minor arcana cards represent the decanates of each zodiacal sign, together with the planet which rules the decanate. To make it easier to understand, the structure of the entire minor arcana is as follows:

The aces of each suit are at the top of the table as the highest and also the most abstract principle of the element. Since the minor arcana are states and events, the Ace of Wands is an intuition, the Pentacle Ace a sensation, the Sword Ace an idea and the Cup Ace a feeling.

The two, three and four of each suit are the decanates of the cardinal signs which initiate the process, the five, six and seven are the fixed signs which sustain and stabilize the process, and the eight, nine and 10 are the mutable signs which lead to culmination and also contain the seeds of change.

Each decanate has a ruling planet which rules either the sign of the decanate or one of the other two signs of the same elemental suit. The three fire signs Aries, Leo and Sagittarius are ruled by Mars, the Sun and Jupiter respectively. These three planets rule the three decanates of the fire signs in different sequences. The first decanate of each sign is ruled by the planet which rules the sign itself. For example, the Wand Two is the first decanate of Aries, ruled by Mars, the planet which rules Aries. The Wand Three is the second decanate of Aries ruled by the planet which rules the next sign in the order of the signs, in this case the next fire sign Leo, ruled by the Sun, and acts like the Sun in Aries astrologically. The Wand Four is the third decanate of Aries, the next fire sign Sagittarius, ruled by Jupiter, so the third decanate of Aries is Jupiter in Aries. The first decanate of Leo is Sun in Leo, the second is Jupiter in Leo and the third is Mars in Leo. The first decanate of Sagittarius is Jupiter in Sagittarius (its ruler), the second decanate is Mars (Aries) in Sagittarius, while the third decanate is the Sun (Leo) in Sagittarius. The same process is followed for each of the suits.

The minor arcana cards are colour-coded using the same sequence as the court cards, from red of Aries to red-violet of Pisces, in the inner circle. Within the circle is a geometric shape made up of the appropriate number of suit symbols. The shapes are:

Ace is a single object, as unity
Two is an opposition of duality and polarity
Three is a triangle of equilibrium and balance
Four is a square of wholeness
Five is a pentangle of humanity and refinement
Six is a Star of David of integrating spirit and matter
Seven is a heptangle of the physical world of phenomena
Eight is two interlocking squares of integration
Nine is three interlocking triangles of dynamic action
Ten is two interlocking pentangles of completion

In the Mandala Astrological Tarot the minor arcana cards are organized first according to their astrological elements and then by their signs. Each card in corresponding to a decanate has a series of days in the year over which it has domain. Everyone has a card which governs the time of their birth. For those with more detailed astrological knowledge of the planets other than the Sun, there are decanates and minor arcana cards of residence for each planet in the horoscope.

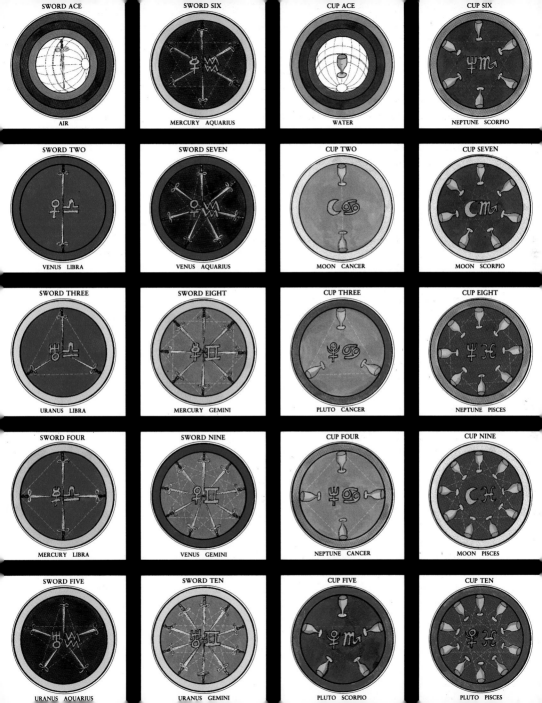

SWORD ACE	SWORD SIX	CUP ACE	CUP SIX
AIR	MERCURY AQUARIUS	WATER	NEPTUNE SCORPIO
SWORD TWO	SWORD SEVEN	CUP TWO	CUP SEVEN
VENUS LIBRA	VENUS AQUARIUS	MOON CANCER	MOON SCORPIO
SWORD THREE	SWORD EIGHT	CUP THREE	CUP EIGHT
URANUS LIBRA	MERCURY GEMINI	PLUTO CANCER	NEPTUNE PISCES
SWORD FOUR	SWORD NINE	CUP FOUR	CUP NINE
MERCURY LIBRA	VENUS GEMINI	NEPTUNE CANCER	MOON PISCES
SWORD FIVE	SWORD TEN	CUP FIVE	CUP TEN
URANUS AQUARIUS	URANUS GEMINI	PLUTO SCORPIO	PLUTO PISCES

THE WAND SUIT
The element Fire
Aries, Leo and Sagittarius

The fire signs initiate each of the three octaves of the horoscope and provide the energy and assertiveness which fuels the zodiac. Essentially the fire signs are expressions of pure spirit manifesting as strong will, aspiration, inspiration, action, courage and daring, rashness and aggression. They are hot, active, masculine, individual, unemotional, dynamic, unstable, extrovert, intuitive. Qualities they produce are creativity, drama, intensity, progress, change, evolution. Feelings they engender are joy, anger, enthusiasm.

WAND ACE – Power in Flashes of Fire

Divination Meanings: Pure, willed energy applied to the conception, birth or commencement of something. Initiating activity.

Reversed Meanings: Blind energy without direction derives from barrenness and sterility. Lack of sexual energy.

WAND ACE

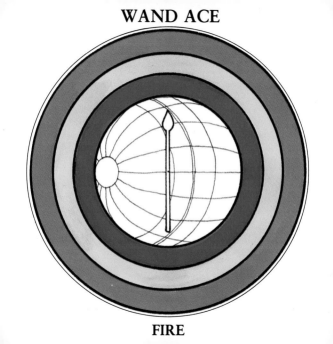

FIRE

WAND TWO, THREE, FOUR

The Lightning of Aries
The Spring Equinox 21 March to 21 April

WAND TWO   21 March to 30 March

Cardinal-Cardinal Fire – First Decan – Mars in Aries

Divination Meanings: A great desire for adventure and domination may create insensitivity to others.

Reversed Meanings: Blind zeal and an overactive desire for independence lead to a waste of energy.

WAND THREE   31 March to 10 April

Fixed-Cardinal Fire – Second Decan – Sun in Aries

Divination Meanings: An ambitious and adventurous disposition leads to alternate rises and falls in career and relationships. Fierce anger expressed regardless of the consequences.

Reversed Meanings: Immaturity leads to a failure of nerve, paralysing willpower.

WAND FOUR   11 April to 21 April

Mutable-Cardinal Fire – Third Decan – Jupiter in Aries

Divination Meanings: Qualities of leadership and organization are used in starting a venture which will be successful.

Reversed Meanings: A lack of balance and resultant moodiness from exaggerated expectations. Premature realization of ideas or plans.

WAND TWO

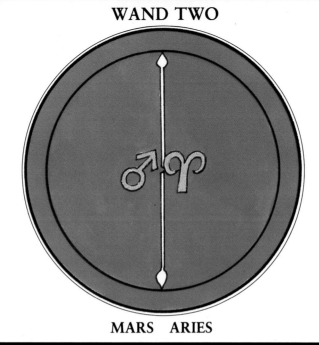

MARS   ARIES

WAND THREE

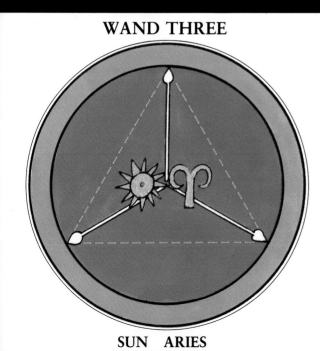

SUN   ARIES

WAND FOUR

JUPITER   ARIES

WAND FIVE, SIX, SEVEN

The Suns of Leo
23 July to 22 August

WAND FIVE   23 July to 1 August

Fixed-Fixed Fire – First Decan – Sun in Leo

Divination Meanings: A noble personality with organizing ability assuming command and authority to accomplish great aspirations. Advancement through one's own ability, warmth and dignity.

Reversed Meanings: Self-centred, pompous and arrogant attitudes and unfounded optimism deny support from others.

WAND SIX   2 August to 11 August

Mutable-Fixed Fire – Second Decan – Jupiter in Leo

Divination Meanings: Self-confidence encourages large-scale planning and eventual victory. Expand and include other views to attract positive foreign influences.

Reversed Meanings: Neglecting the inner life, self-admiration, vanity and cunning.

WAND SEVEN   12 August to 22 August

Cardinal-Fixed Fire – Third Decan – Mars in Leo

Divination Meanings: Enterprising and assured formative energy manifests as strength and valour.

Reversed Meanings: Too much passionate but undirected love of self requires a great demand for self-control.

WAND FIVE

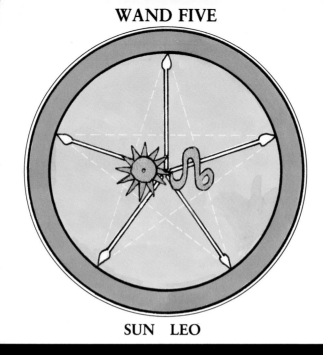

SUN   LEO

WAND SIX

JUPITER   LEO

WAND SEVEN

MARS · LEO

WAND EIGHT, NINE, TEN

The Rainbows of Sagittarius
23 November to 21 December

WAND EIGHT   23 November to 2 December

Mutable-Mutable Fire – First Decan – Jupiter in Sagittarius

Divination Meanings: An optimistic belief in the future through systemic leadership and inspiration. Prophetic and inspirational ideas must wait for recognition.

Reversed Meanings: An excess of vainglory and egotism combines with overt self-importance to undermine collective projects.

WAND NINE   3 December to 12 December

Cardinal-Mutable Fire – Second Decan – Mars in Sagittarius

Divination Meanings: Gaining victory after the application of great effort in physical and spiritual directions. Highly idealistic motives need a basis in tangible reality.

Reversed Meanings: A lack of diplomacy and understanding of others' views can generate friction and opposition, and lead to throwing energy away unnecessarily.

WAND TEN   13 December to 21 December

Fixed-Mutable Fire – Third Decan – Sun in Sagittarius

Divination Meanings: Goals may be achieved through the power of positive thinking, visualization and affirmation. A dual nature requires both religious and material objectives to be complete.

Reversed Meanings: Jumping to irrational conclusions. Making unrealistic decisions which are oppressive, but contain the seeds for change.

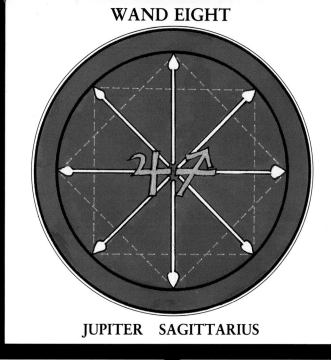

WAND EIGHT

JUPITER   SAGITTARIUS

WAND NINE

MARS   SAGITTARIUS

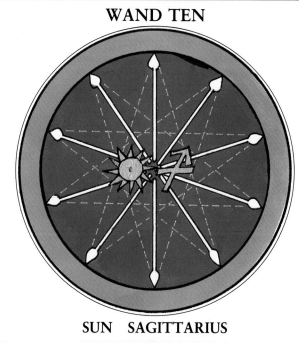

WAND TEN

SUN   SAGITTARIUS

THE PENTACLE SUIT

The element Earth
Taurus, Virgo and Capricorn

The earth signs are the manifestation into physical form of the energy generated by the spirit and create, stabilize and sustain the physical bodies. Essentially the earth signs are physical: practical, material, conservative, possessive, secure, industrious and thrifty. They are cold, passive, feminine, individual, emotional, static, stable, introvert and sensitive. Qualities they express are common sense, structure, resistance to change, tangibility, emotional reliability. Shadow qualities of earth signs are pig-headedness, intransigence, excessive passivity, overly practical, unfeeling, distant, materialistic obsessions and a general resistance to movement and change.

PENTACLE ACE – Power in Mountains of Earth

Divination Meanings: An inheritance of earthly power and wealth. Good health and abundance.

Reversed Meanings: Loss of power and possessions taxes an unstable material situation.

PENTACLE ACE

EARTH

PENTACLE TWO, THREE, FOUR

The Mountains of Capricorn
The Winter Solstice, 22 December to 19 January

PENTACLE TWO 22 December to 30 December

Cardinal-Cardinal Earth – First Decan – Saturn in Capricorn

Divination Meanings: A very serious attitude to material security and structure leads to coldness and neglect of others' feelings. Concentration upon strength of will.

Reversed Meanings: Anxiety and detachment through materialistic values. Self-willed. Egocentric.

PENTACLE THREE 31 December to 9 January

Fixed-Cardinal Earth – Second Decan – Venus in Capricorn

Divination Meanings: Constancy and faithfulness in relationships that require responsibility to those older and more experienced. Feeling a need for great self-control.

Reversed Meanings: Too much self-control and introspection produce a dreary and unsatisfying relationship. Danger of disappointment and separation.

PENTACLE FOUR 10 January to 19 January

Mutable-Cardinal Earth – Third Decan – Mercury in Capricorn

Divination Meanings: A clear, practical and methodical mind is applied to serious problems which have earthly power as a goal.

Reversed Meanings: A tendency to be too slow and steady, intolerant of invention and overly serious. Excessive craftiness and cunning can be isolating and melancholic.

PENTACLE TWO

SATURN   CAPRICORN

PENTACLE THREE

VENUS   CAPRICORN

PENTACLE FOUR

MERCURY   CAPRICORN

PENTACLE FIVE, SIX, SEVEN

The Plains of Taurus
22 April to 20 May

PENTACLE FIVE   22 April to 1 May

Fixed-Fixed Earth – First Decan – Venus in Taurus

Divination Meanings: Personal attraction and emotional constancy gains the attention of beautiful people, but understanding of non-material things can bring even greater rewards.

Reversed Meanings: Loss of possessions through jealousy and intense strain may lead to a period of spiritual growth.

PENTACLE SIX   2 May to 11 May

Mutable-Fixed Earth – Second Decan – Mercury in Taurus

Divination Meanings: Outstanding decisions require much thought, planning and deliberation. Hard work leads to a greater ease of expression through attention to form and detail.

Reversed Meanings: One-sided or overly materialistic views are a limitation and need to be changed in order to overcome lethargy and inactivity.

PENTACLE SEVEN   12 May to 20 May

Cardinal-Fixed Earth – Third Decan – Saturn in Taurus

Divination Meanings: Potential success is prevented by unrealistic speculations and material inertia, which must be overcome by discipline. A conservative outlook and controlled feelings combine to form material impotence.

Reversed Meanings: Stubbornness in maintaining obsolete attitudes which limit growth and create anxiety and worries.

PENTACLE FIVE

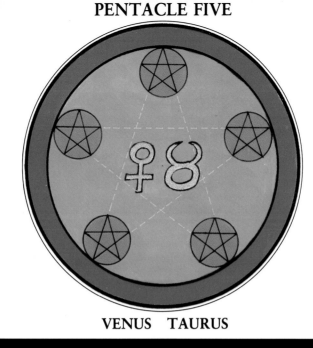

VENUS   TAURUS

PENTACLE SIX

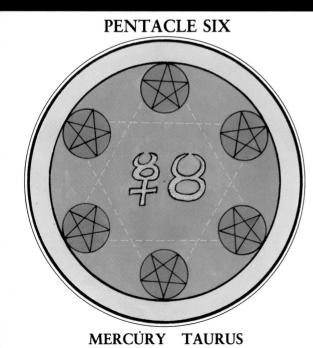

MERCURY   TAURUS

PENTACLE SEVEN

SATURN   TAURUS

PENTACLE EIGHT, NINE, TEN

The Fields of Virgo
23 August to 22 September

PENTACLE EIGHT   23 August to 1 September

Mutable-Mutable Earth – First Decan – Mercury in Virgo

Divination Meanings: Logical, practical and detailed attention is applied skilfully to material matters. A thirst for knowledge and understanding is expressed as expertise but is limited by little facility in seeing the whole.

Reversed Meanings: Difficulties in collaborating and a tendency to internalize all outer difficulties make for nervousness, stress and psychosomatic illnesses.

PENTACLE NINE   2 September to 11 September

Cardinal-Mutable Earth – Second Decan – Saturn in Virgo

Divination Meanings: Awareness leads to the need to adjust goals to conform to real circumstances. Prudent action avoids criticism and fulfils responsibilities.

Reversed Meanings: A pedantic and nagging nature acts alone and generates misunderstandings which confuse and alienate others.

PENTACLE TEN   12 September to 22 September

Fixed-Mutable Earth – Third Decan – Venus in Virgo

Divination Meanings: Too much analysis of feelings and criticism of loved ones makes for self-consciousness, inhibitions and indecisive relationships. Things look better than they are.

Reversed Meanings: A fastidious and cold exterior can frustrate and inhibit social contacts which are inwardly necessary.

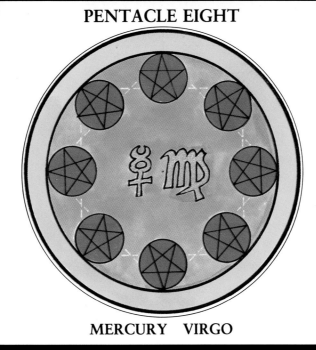

PENTACLE EIGHT

MERCURY VIRGO

PENTACLE NINE

SATURN VIRGO

PENTACLE TEN

VENUS VIRGO

THE SWORD SUIT

The element Air
Gemini, Libra and Aquarius

The air signs are unstable, wilful and self-expressive and make relationships possible. They are expressions of pure mind manifesting as strong ideas, perception, alertness, versatility, observation, cooperation, compatibility and nervousness. They are cold, active, masculine, related, unemotional, dynamic, unstable, extrovert, thinking and detached. Qualities they express are humane, detached, dualistic, vacillating, alert, logical, quickness in mind and body. Shadow qualities of air signs are their abstraction and distance, lack of intimacy, intellectual criticism, ambiguity and lack of constancy.

SWORD ACE – Power in Winds of Air

Divination Meanings: Communication of ideas for their own sake requires discriminating intellect. Definite and certain attitudes.

Reversed Meanings: Trust consistently betrayed leads to misunderstanding and a breakdown of communication. Difficulties with intimacy.

SWORD ACE

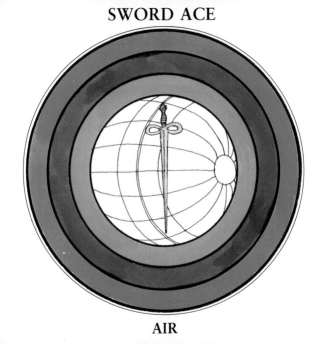

AIR

SWORD TWO, THREE, FOUR

The Winds of Libra
Autumnal Equinox, 23 September to 22 October

SWORD TWO   23 September to 2 October

Cardinal-Cardinal Air – First Decan – Venus in Libra

Divination Meanings: A harmonious relationship is founded on art, love and perfect balance.

Reversed Meanings: Scattered affections created by overidealizing the loved one.

SWORD THREE   3 October to 12 October

Fixed-Cardinal Air – Second Decan – Uranus in Libra

Divination Meanings: A focus on creative interests of great originality lead to compromised relationships. Unexpected material success through contracts or legal action.

Reversed Meanings: Ignoring creative possibilities leads to dissatisfaction with routine and a desire to break away in rebellion.

SWORD FOUR   13 October to 22 October

Mutable-Cardinal Air – Third Decan – Mercury in Libra

Divination Meanings: Creative thinking within already existing patterns often avoids unpleasant but critical issues.

Reversed Meanings: A lack of tact and a tendency to overintellectualize.

SWORD TWO

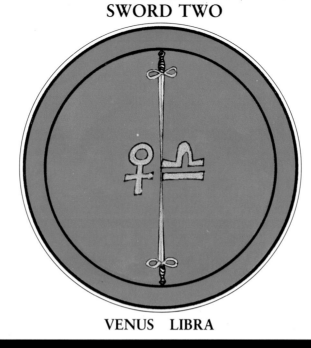

VENUS   LIBRA

SWORD THREE

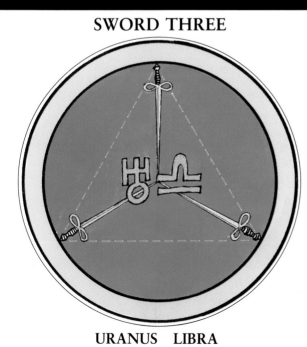

URANUS   LIBRA

SWORD FOUR

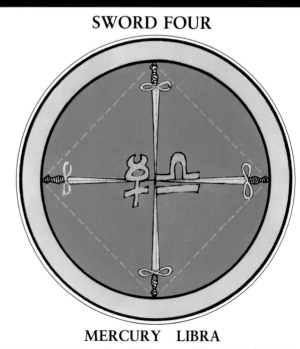

MERCURY   LIBRA

SWORD FIVE, SIX, SEVEN

The Clouds of Aquarius
20 January to 18 February

SWORD FIVE   20 January to 29 January

Fixed-Fixed Air – First Decan – Uranus in Aquarius

Divination Meanings: Original thoughts combined with eccentric actions begin and end relationships suddenly. Progressive attitudes attract indirect help from others.

Reversed Meanings: Unreliable and unpredictable. Irrational feelings and rebellious behaviour are exaggerated and magnified.

SWORD SIX   30 January to 8 February

Mutable-Fixed Air – Second Decan – Mercury in Aquarius

Divination Meanings: New experiences and progressive thinking in group situations must be judged quickly and then stabilized for maximum effect. An awakening of the conscious mind inventively.

Reversed Meanings: A tendency to be too idealistic when confronted with reality leads to loneliness and isolation. Unconventional behaviour can lead to antagonism and chaos.

SWORD SEVEN   9 February to 18 February

Cardinal-Fixed Air – Third Decan – Venus in Aquarius

Divination Meanings: Unconventional and individual ideas about relationships bring enjoyment of social life but a continual need for independence. Partnerships are unstable, tending to begin and also end suddenly and without notice.

Reversed Meanings: Promiscuous and eccentric sexuality creates a joyful life fraught with uncertainty and emotional chaos.

SWORD FIVE

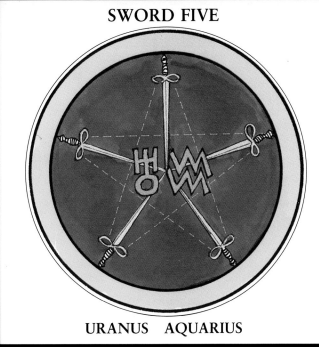

URANUS   AQUARIUS

SWORD SIX

MERCURY   AQUARIUS

SWORD SEVEN

VENUS   AQUARIUS

SWORD EIGHT, NINE, TEN

The Vibrations of Gemini
21 May to 20 June

SWORD EIGHT   21 May to 31 May

Mutable-Mutable Air – First Decan – Mercury in Gemini

Divination Meanings: A continual love of variety and constant change can create beneficial work situations if enough concentration is applied. Mental originality with difficulty in focusing on practical applications.

Reversed Meanings: Too much complexity creates confusion, stress and sudden outbursts of anger. Accident prone and inconstant.

SWORD NINE   1 June to 10 June

Cardinal-Mutable Air – Second Decan – Venus in Gemini

Divination Meanings: Desire for variety in social life and work can be unsettling. It is necessary to be accommodating and open with friends, but feelings of loyalty should be sustained.

Reversed Meanings: Despair caused by inconstancy or resignation in affections, and bizarre values in emotional contacts.

SWORD TEN   11 June to 20 June

Fixed-Mutable Air – Third Decan – Uranus in Gemini

Divination Meanings: Quick comprehension of organizational matters leads to easy boredom and restlessness. The need to control intellect and apply will power to real needs.

Reversed Meanings: Scattering energy in a disjointed fashion makes for confusion and relationships which are insecure.

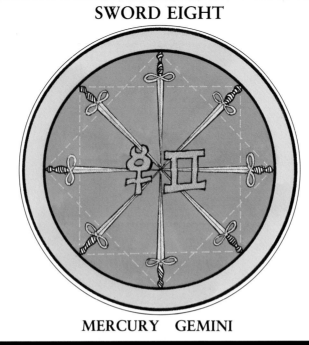

SWORD EIGHT

MERCURY   GEMINI

SWORD NINE

VENUS   GEMINI

SWORD TEN

URANUS   GEMINI

THE CUP SUIT

The element Water
Cancer, Scorpio and Pisces

The water signs are the most difficult to define, being subjective, personal and receptive to outer influences. Essentially the water signs are value systems or feelings which are often unexpressed or expressed as emotional, sensitive, mediumistic, impressionable, imaginative, psychic, secretive and visionary. They are cold, passive, feminine, dependent, emotional, changeable, unstable, introvert and feeling. Qualities they generate are romantic, indulgent, expressive, valued, imaginative, devotional and erotic. Shadow qualities are two-sided, scatty, overemotional, obsessive, hypochondriac, psychosomatic and overly influenced by others.

CUP ACE – Power in Rains of Water

Divination Meanings: Strong instinctive feelings of love and devotion at the commencement of an affair. Absorbing others' emotions.

Reversed Meanings: Emotional inconstancy produces insensitivity and coldness of unrequited love.

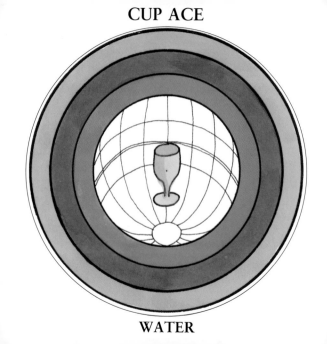

CUP TWO, THREE, FOUR

The Rains of Cancer
The Summer Solstice 21 June to 22 July

CUP TWO   21 June to 1 July

Cardinal-Cardinal Water – First Decan – Moon in Cancer

Divination Meanings: Emotional strength and security due to a simple, basic family nature. Sensitivity to moods is psychic.

Reversed Meanings: Emotional instability and family problems caused by insecurity and too much dependency upon others.

CUP THREE   2 July to 11 July

Fixed-Cardinal Water – Second Decan – Pluto in Cancer

Divination Meanings: An emotional change of mind discovered through contemplation leads to the need for withdrawal. Great tension at home creates emotional flare-ups and a change in attitude to loved ones.

Reversed Meanings: Emotional breakdown caused by a resistance to confront an important issue.

CUP FOUR   12 July to 22 August

Mutable-Cardinal Water – Third Decan – Neptune in Cancer

Divination Meanings: A deeply sensitive and feeling nature is easily susceptible to instability and can be misled. Clairvoyance subjected to wilful directions by idealism.

Reversed Meanings: A clouded reality can hurt by taking in more than can be understood. Suffering from disappointment.

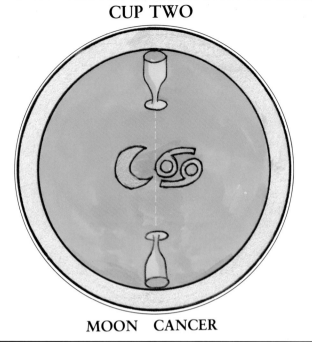

CUP TWO

MOON   CANCER

CUP THREE

PLUTO   CANCER

CUP FOUR

NEPTUNE   CANCER

CUP FIVE, SIX, SEVEN

The Sea of Scorpio
23 October to 22 November

CUP FIVE   23 October to 1 November

Fixed-Fixed Water – First Decan – Pluto in Scorpio

Divination Meanings: Courage and the drive to succeed at all costs. Strong unconscious pressures influence others negatively.

Reversed Meanings: Tragic events due to the inability to change enough. Losses despite apparently positive circumstances.

CUP SIX   2 November to 12 November

Mutable-Fixed Water – Second Decan – Neptune in Scorpio

Divination Meanings: Intuition leading to separation. Great emotional intensity and pressure create tension in sexual life. Receiving psychic impulses can lead to beneficial moves.

Reversed Meanings: Depression caused by difficult and stressed mental states. Emotional turmoil disrupts stability, but there is the potential for regeneration.

CUP SEVEN   13 November to 1 November

Cardinal-Fixed Water – Third Decan – Moon in Scorpio

Divination Meanings: Taking personal adventures and affairs so seriously that the resultant jealousy is dangerous. Need to balance psychic sensitivity with emotional stability through honest and truthful relationships.

Reversed Meanings: Stubborn domination of relationships is damaging and disappointing. Lacking frankness and honesty is paralysing.

CUP FIVE

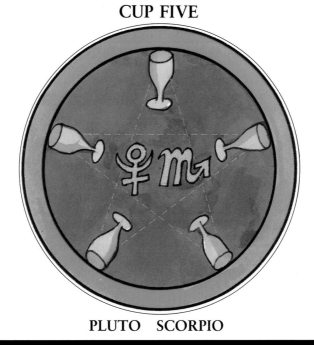

PLUTO   SCORPIO

CUP SIX

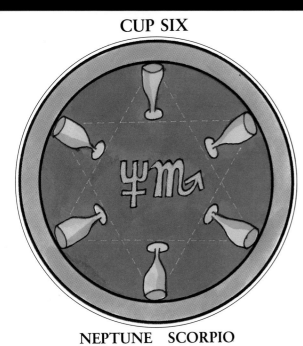

NEPTUNE   SCORPIO

CUP SEVEN

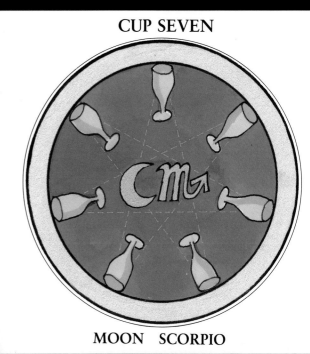

MOON   SCORPIO

CUP EIGHT, NINE, TEN

The Pools of Pisces
19 February to 20 March

CUP EIGHT   19 February to 28 February

Mutable-Mutable Water – First Decan – Neptune in Pisces

Divination Meanings: Separation from the outer world leads to artistic reverie, fantasies and idealistic visions which do not have a realistic foundation. Open to emotional blackmail.

Reversed Meanings: Craving alcohol, drugs and sex as an escape from dealing with self. Hidden pathological tendencies.

CUP NINE   1 March to 10 March

Cardinal-Mutable Water – Second Decan – Moon in Pisces

Divination Meanings: Extreme psychic sensitivity and moodiness generates a danger of being badly influenced. Hopeful of positive feelings from partners.

Reversed Meanings: Psychologically vulnerable to emotional pressure from loved ones. Dominance of irrational emotions.

CUP TEN   11 March to 21 March

Fixed-Mutable Water – Third Decan – Pluto in Pisces

Divination Meanings: Supreme artistic activity comes from unconscious drives which have viable means of expression. Universal feelings must be translated into real experience.

Reversed Meanings: Tempted to revert to previously debauched positions. Ego-tripping becomes dangerous and stressful.

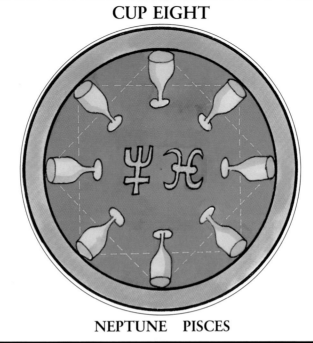

CUP EIGHT

NEPTUNE   PISCES

CUP NINE

MOON   PISCES

CUP TEN

PLUTO   PISCES

Chapter 5

〜◆〜

INTERPRETING
TAROT

A most important question is: How does divination work? At each instant in the universe of time and space the Creator modifies everything that exists through an invisible web which forms a foundation for the destiny of the world. This form-generating field can be tapped in a number of ways, both spontaneous and formal.

Spontaneous connections with the inner workings of the world include access to the unconscious through dreams, psychic flashes, synchronicities and visualizations. A favourable ground for receiving such essential communications about the way the world acts can be created through meditation, yoga, active imagination, guided imagery, magical practices and the mantic arts, all of which encourage an opening of the psyche or soul to higher energies within which we all exist.

Mantic arts are ways of tapping into the universal process at a certain time and place. Often the specific information must be received through a symbol system which is created as a channel. Early mantic arts were created to meet the demand for mirrors of the self in the world. For example, if one mentally defines an area of the sky as a sacred space or zone, and sets conventions which allow one to define the present or future by the way in which anything enters the zone, a mantic art has been created. The mantic art therefore exists both in the outer world and within the mind and psyche of the practitioner. One convention could be that if anything, whether it be bird or cloud, enters from above the issue will imply conscious response, while if from below instinctive response. A cloud would show a vague issue, while a large black crow flying diagonally across the imaginary screen from bottom to top would imply powerful negative influences of which one should become conscious.

From this basic start, an entire system could be developed, taking any possible manifestations into consideration.

The ancients developed many such systems, a few of which are still used in the present day, and many of which are in the process of being rediscovered and popularized. Two striking examples are the Chinese I Ching and the Nordic runes. The I Ching (The Book of Changes) is a mathematically based oracle used by dividing and subdividing yarrow stalks to generate hexagrams composed of six stacked solid or broken lines. The resultant 64 possibilities have been carefully related to the entire range of human activities and archetypal behaviour patterns. One hexagram changes subtly to another, creating many permutations and very accurate forecasting. The Chinese believe that chance occurrences are true to reality, and that the bringing into focus of chance events is highly significant. The yarrow stalks are spiritual agencies which act mysteriously to give meaningful answers.

A modern explanation is that consciousness of a question affects and is affected by what is. Jung called the interaction synchronicity, by which he meant that there is more than a coincidence between events in space and time which have apparently the same meaning. He postulated the interdependence of outer events with the inner subjective psychic states of an observer. In this viewpoint, which is increasingly but reluctantly being accepted by some modern physicists, each event in the universe is linked to every other event, and therefore the throwing of coins or separating of yarrow stalks are valid ways for gaining access to the world process at a given moment. The mechanism by which contact is initiated is the Question.

The Question

The essence of any oracular system is the question. In order to use the I Ching, the runes, flipping a coin or tarot cards, there should be a question, either formally stated or implied. Beyond the wish for an answer, the question is a focusing of the mind and heart. It is to this important issue that some thought must be devoted.

Often one is counselled not to do readings for oneself. Many tarot authorities recommend that the question should be known only to the questioner, not to the interpreter (reader). The implication is that the interpreter is only a vehicle or medium, and that knowledge of the question could lead to prejudice or distortion. These viewpoints, however, are antique in that the divination process takes place between aspects of being within the individual. Outward events and questions which arise from them are only devices to which the personality responds to the message of the soul. A primary function of the divination process is to take what is at first implicit or inherent and to make it explicit or meaningful – which is to link outward events with inner understanding, or to integrate parts of oneself which are separate or confused. Out of the duality between the questioner and the reader, a higher third view will emerge through the medium of the cards.

It is basic wisdom that questions are more important than answers. The reason for this is that questions typically open up reality, while answers close options down and put an end to an issue. It is therefore essential to be aware of the way in which questions are asked, and what can be learned by them. To begin a tarot reading with a request for a question is often very perplexing, yet a client will probably have asked for a reading with some issue in mind. The more precise the question, the more carefully the individual has considered the issue. While many people want very precise answers, their questions are often vague and indeterminate. A primary principle in tarot is that the quality of the answer is related to, and determined by, the quality of the question. If an individual cannot define clearly what it is that he or she wishes to know, then the process of discovery of the question will often be a primary part of the answer. When a question is clearly expressed, ways to arrive at an answer are often inherent in it, and the process of discovery can be more valuable than the answer.

All mantic arts have as their central function a focusing of the psyche and mind upon itself. Coins, yarrow stalks or tarot cards, as well as the reader, are merely intermediaries between an individual and his or her inner self. In this sense, the oracle is a mirror reflecting the issue back to the questioner. This places a very great importance upon the question. Learning to interpret tarot cards encourages the process within the reader as well as performing that function for the questioner.

The first stage of the tarot reading is for the questioner to define the question so that his or her conscious mind is directed to the core of the issue. The statement of the question must make obvious what is implied.

Often, the phrasing of the question carries a good indication of the degree of resistance to an issue. When the presenting question is: What is going on with me? it is clear that the individual has no idea where and who he or she is, and is probably resisting looking at the situation. The object of the reading would therefore be to initiate the inward-looking process. To follow with a request for a more tightly formulated question encourages a closer look at the issue, to sense the quality of the present moment, and to ask from which issue the question has arisen. The process of determining the question is very important. Lack of direction is often caused by losing contact with the present time. In this case it is often necessary to start with a question such as: Where are you right now? What are you feeling right now? and if the question involves others, whose image arises right now?

The first function of the tarot reader is to bring the querent to present time.

The remainder of this chapter will show how to establish the quality of the present moment, and then to expand the complexity of the questions and the types of card layouts with which you may address them. The progression will be from the simplest reading to the most complex so that you can grow as you become more familiar with the tarot. The first types of readings will have the added function of being ways to become familiar with the cards. In the process, various aspects of tarot divination will be addressed, such as the way in which the cards are to be kept, shuffled and laid out, as well as the way to interpret them.

The Practice of Tarot

There are many 'old wives tales' about tarot, consistent with its historical connections with Gypsy fortune-tellers, and many concern the basic attitude to the process of tarot itself. Many believe that the cards are magnetically attuned to their owner, and that no one else should handle or use the cards once they enter one's ownership. Along the same lines it is often suggested that the cards should be kept wrapped in pure silk to 'protect the vibrations' of the cards. While accepting that tarot can be part of a ritual, and that it is quite important to establish a ritual for using the cards, it is also important that the way in which you treat tarot is appropriate to your own needs. There are no universal rules of tarot divination – it is essential to create and concentrate energies to the task at hand.

By freeing the mind from external influences it is possible to see more clearly the truth of things. Tarot is a tool for focusing the mind to a particular issue, restraining its tendency to wander off target, and for learning to control the mind. There are certain practices which encourage these goals.

The act of reading tarot cards should be considered a ritual. There are times when it is appropriate to read the cards, and other times when it is not. It is important that issues deserving concentration and effort be accorded the right situations. Therefore, it is not a good idea to use the tarot cards for play or fun, but rather with the intention of seriously asking the cards for symbols to further understanding. Listen to your inner voice about whether or not to read the tarot cards.

The ritual which develops for using tarot cards is individual, and is built up over time in a form which is appropriate for each person. The only important precept is that once a ritual is developed that it is followed closely each time the tarot cards are consulted. In order to test one's ability to use the cards, and to discover more about them a few aids are encouraged, but not essential.

The first is to keep the cards in a protected place, a place which is special, so that they partake of your deeper, higher inner Self and act as its vehicle.

It is helpful to keep a diary to record the time, place and other details of readings. This has a multiple function: it provides you with a record of your improving perceptions of the process, and your progress in understanding. The entries may be made as you wish, but it is helpful to draw the layout of the cards, your reactions to them, and whether the symbols and images received were relevant or not to the issues at hand.

Meditation on the question and the process itself is a helpful prelude to reading the cards. Take a few minutes, be quiet, close your eyes, and concentrate upon stilling your mind. Let the cares of the day slip away, and open yourself to receive higher energies and intuitions, which will pass through to you if you are open enough. Try to gather your mental powers and bring them to bear on the mantic process concerned.

The Story

As with the interpretation of dreams, the process of translating the images received from the cards, or from their descriptions in this book, into your own vocabulary and life at a particular time is very revealing. It is best to develop your own process for interpreting the cards. The cards do not have an absolute meaning apart from your own experience of them. It is even appropriate to understand a specific card differently each time it occurs in a reading. The card remains the same, the images and symbols are the same, but the situation in which it is drawn is always different. Feel free to interpret the images or meanings in the way they seem right to you at the time. Associate freely upon anything which comes into your mind.

The best way to interpret tarot is to treat the process as one would in the telling of a story about the person or issue in question. Each card interpreted in sequence becomes a catalyst for images which further the plot, add qualities to the cast of characters and make the meaning of the story more specific.

All events in our lives are carried and transmitted as stories. When we meet someone for the first time, we tell them stories, selected consciously or unconsciously, which show or obscure what we are or may be, and which display our qualities to the best advantage. In return, we hear their stories. As relationships continue, more and more stories are told and the entire picture is pieced together until the whole person begins to emerge.

Stories never remain the same, but evolve to fit changing circumstances. Our parents' stories about our early childhood are told and retold so many times that eventually they emerge as thoroughly edited versions conveying what our parents want us to believe. The chances are that situations which presented them in an unfortunate light have been lost or altered. This is human nature. In the same way we qualify our own stories to make ourselves appear in a more favourable light, or even for the sake of a better story. To a certain extent, we are defined by the way we choose and tell stories, and how we accept and work with the stories of others. All these mechanisms are important to tarot reading.

The question, or the personality of the questioner, is the departure point for the creation of a story which may describe what is happening at the present moment, may be a reconstruction of the past, or an extension into the future. The questioner sets the scope of the story by the question, and the reader constructs possible plots and their resolution. The ability to get to the core of the reading is valuable in tarot as well as in life.

Shuffling and Laying Out the Cards

It is essential that the cards are thoroughly shuffled into a homogeneous mix before you consult the tarot. Ask the questioner to take the cards and shuffle them until they are well mixed. As will soon be clear, it is also important that the cards are not all in the same orientation. Of course, with time and constant use, the deck will become totally mixed and the cards oriented in all four directions. If the cards have been put together upright for any reason, it is a good idea to shuffle them thoroughly before presenting them to the questioner.

When the cards are given to the questioner to be shuffled, request a moment of silence to centre the mind. Explain your individual procedure for the reading, and ask the person to concentrate on the question, if indeed a question has been asked. While meditating upon and considering these issues, he or she should shuffle the cards.

Once the cards are thoroughly shuffled and the questioner feels composed, comfortable with the question and settled, the deck should be placed face down upon the table. Cut the deck approximately in half, then put it together again. Repeat this process three times. The deck is now ready for laying out.

When the cards are laid out on a table for a reading, it is essential that each card is removed from the top of the deck and placed down in the same way. Whether the cards are taken and turned from left to right, or upside down from the deck is a matter of choice, but it is important that the same process is repeated for every card. This is to ensure the correct orientation of each card. Eventually you will discover a way of turning the cards over which is consistent and feels right for you.

Card Orientation

Virtually all traditional and modern tarot decks are rectangular in shape. As a result, a card may be laid down in either an upright position in relation to the reader, or upside down. The duality is usually expressed by each card having two opposite meanings. The upright card is understood as being strong, positive or beneficial, while the upside down or reversed card is weak, negative or malefic. In reality both sides of every card act in each case. The positive-negative alignments are therefore quite contrary to logic, and truer as complementary qualities.

In the Mandala Astrological Tarot the issue of orientation is profoundly altered because the cards are square. This means that each card may be laid in any one of four possible orientations: i.e. with the title upright, reversed, to the left or to the right. While this at first seems an even greater complication, it allows a much wider range of interpretations. The key to the orientation of square cards is the structure of the astrological horoscope.

The horoscope circle is divided into 12 sections, but the most important points are the horizontal and vertical axes, called the angles. The point at the top of the vertical meridian is the *MC*, equivalent to the position of the sun at noon, which represents ego consciousness and spiritual awareness. Its opposite point, the *IC* (Immum Coeli = lower midheaven) represents the heart of the unconscious. The horizontal axis faces east-west. The eastern horizon is the *ASC* (Ascendant), which is the personality or self, while the western horizon is the *DSC* (Descendant), one's partner, the outside world or the not-self. A simple and effective orientation results from using the Cardinal Cross.

When a card is upright, the influence of the card is conscious. When a card is reversed, the influence of the card is unconscious. When a card leans to the left towards the ASC, the influence emanates from the personality. When a card leans to the right towards the DSC, the influence emanates from one's partner or the outside world.

To give an example, the Fool upright is the awareness that one is naive and innocent, when reversed there is a lack of awareness of such innocence; to the left is an innocent personality, while to the right an innocent partner. Each orientation qualifies the meaning of the card and reveals to whom the influence should be attributed. You can practice by taking any one of the major arcana cards, looking up its basic meaning in the text, and trying to interpret it in each of the four orientations.

One-Card Spread

The Daily Card is one of the best tools for learning with the Mandala Astrological Tarot. Each day, preferably at the same time, concentrate on the day, meditate to still your mind, shuffle the cards, cut them, and when you have placed the pack on the table in front of you, turn the top card over. That card will show the quality of the day or of the moment. Look at the card, its imagery, its colour, the sign or planet which rules it, to determine what inspires you. When you have finished concentrating on the image, turn to the appropriate page of the book and read its meaning. Write down the card chosen, your interpretation of the meaning and how it is relevant or irrelevant to your present situation.

The card acts as the Significator which alludes to both the questioner and the question.

You can qualify the one-card reading by putting a question to the card, or by referring it to someone else. You can ask, for example: What will my boss be like today? If you get the Tower he or she will tend to be angry and destructive, while the Wheel of Fortune reversed would show that he or she has old-fashioned attitudes which could create conflict. The Moon leaning to the right would show the presence of obstacles originating from previous partnerships. In these examples the meanings are altered according to the position of the cards. In a similar manner the same procedure may be used to qualify your understanding of the matter. With this in mind, the anger of the Tower may be the first stage of a transformation; the old-fashionedness of the Wheel of Fortune can be overcome by adopting the larger view that there are positive values in old viewpoints, and that recognizing obsolete attitudes leads to revitalizing them; the past obstacles of the leaning Moon may be brought to the surface (upright) and cleaned up, allowing relief from duality. Every card carries the seeds of its own resolution.

In the beginning it is usually easier to use only major arcana cards which have quite definite and clear meanings and then, when you feel comfortable with them, graduate on to the entire deck with the court cards and minor arcana.

Remember that the major arcana cards are the most powerful and have archetypal meanings, the court cards show people with whom you are likely to have contact, and the minor arcana cards are situations which you are likely to experience.

The Crossing Challenge

A device often used in tarot is to place a card on top of the Significator to cross it, and its function is much like having a cross to bear. The Crossing card is a challenge to the questioner or question, which must be cleared up before understanding or resolution ensues, or it is a blockage which must be dissolved or removed. As the cards are square, the Crossing card should be placed over the Significator at a slight diagonal, so that it only partially obscures the Significator and both can be seen.

The Crossing is very important. When the Significator and Crossing seem to agree with each other, for example when they are both of the same suit, such as the Sword Five and the Sword Queen, the question and challenge are sympathetic and any obstacles may be overcome relatively easily. Likewise, when the Tower (the card of Mars and the Emperor) and the sign Aries, which is ruled by Mars, are drawn as Significator and Crossing there would also be agreement, the Tower ruling the Emperor. When there is a major arcana card as a Crossing and a minor arcana card as Significator, the implication would be that the obstacles are much more powerful than the questioner, at the moment.

Major arcana cards appearing in either position show powerful archetypal patterns in action. Court cards appearing often lead to identifying a person or behavioural pattern which is significant. Minor arcana cards are situations or mechanisms in operation.

The Crossing is the obstacle preventing the questioner or question from manifesting, but also contains clues about the way to remove the blockage. All tarot cards contain the seed of the circumstances they describe which may lead to resolution. Therefore, always look beneath the apparent situation indicated to the core to discover what the event or question reveals about the questioner.

Past, Present and Future

All readings emanate from the central Significator, the questioner and the question, both of which are simply expressions of the Self. The Crossing card is the challenge or obstacle within the self, or an indication of the separation of self from the issue at hand. The Significator is present in every type of tarot spread and the addition of other cards elaborate the basic one-card layout. The format of the rest of the spreads shown in the book will be built around the Significator or the Significator and Crossing, and illustrated as such throughout.

The organization of spreads follows the astrological form already described:

above = consciousness	= South/Noon
below = unconsciousness	= North/Midnight
left = personality (and the past)	= East/Sunrise
right = partner (and the future)	= West/Sunset

Cards placed above the Significator show conscious influences, below the Significator unconscious influences, to the left the past history, and to the right the future.

The primary movement (past, present and future) is from left to right for simple spreads, as in the illustration on the facing page. For more complex spreads, the movement revolves in a counter-clockwise direction starting with the far left, the place of the personality.

The Past, Present and Future spread is easy to learn and virtually self-explanatory. It is appropriate for most situations or questions, and uses a basic sequence in time as its core. The position of the Significator becomes the central card of the three.

When the cards are shuffled, remind the questioner to meditate on, or think about, his or her circumstances projected in time. Once again the spread will reveal the evolution of a situation or question which also contains the seed of resolution.

Place the cards down, starting with the central card, the Present, and following with the card to the left, the Past, and ending with the card to the right, the Future.

The *Past* card is the personality of the questioner, the development of the situation leading up to the present which is significant and bears upon the issue at hand. In the past causes which require effects have been produced. The past is the raw material upon which the Self acts to grow and evolve.

The *Present* card is the existing situation, what is going on right now, and also the course of action required. The present may represent an inner or outer blockage, a challenge, a cure, a person who is involved, or a behaviour pattern which is being enacted.

The *Future* card is the outcome of the situation, which is in turn the seed of a new situation which will evolve from the present.

The important quality of the Past, Present and Future spread is to discover and transmit the process which underlies the apparent outer reality of the situation. All events in life have meaning which, when understood and integrated, provide sustenance for renewed growth of the self on its path to join with the universal Self.

Upright cards are consciousness of the part of the process indicated, reversed cards are areas of which the questioner is unconscious. Cards leaning to the left or right show whether the issue originates or stems from the personality or the partner as symbolic of the outside world.

A sample reading follows, using only the major arcana. The question: Is the prominent politician a Russian spy? The cards as placed are:

Past	Present	Future
Justice	Fool	Magician
left side	upright	reversed

The card in the past is Justice leaning to the left side, the place of the personality. The meaning of the Justice card is 'using influence in political and personal spheres. Deliberation is required in order to recognize that the cause for the imbalance is within'. The politician himself has been always within the law before, in fact upholding the law, but has had political and personal relationships with Russians.

The card in the Present position is the Fool upright. The meaning of the Fool is 'the beginning of an adventure; awakening perception; irrationality; taking the initiative without considering the consequences'. While disclosures are being made about the politician's present behaviour, certain new information will become available. Although the charges are irrational, it may be that he made contact without fully realizing the implications of his actions, rather than with treasonable intention.

The Future card is the reversed Magician. The meaning of the Magician reversed is 'appearances hide reality, leading to seduction by power'. What the politican and his apparently law-abiding past show is only an appearance hiding the real issue, that he was seduced by the potential of power. The balancing act of the Magician is breaking down, and the politician is a spy.

The reversed card in the Future position shows a dramatic and unexpected change in circumstances from expectations, and the imagery of the Magician juggling many objects in the air upside down clearly implies that the balance has been upset, leading to conviction. The upright Fool in the centre shows that there is a question of foolish behaviour of which the politician was aware.

The underlying process is the sequence that has led from Justice to the Fool, ending with an upset Magician. Had the last card been upright, the outcome would be totally different, and the juggling act would have been successful.

The Celtic Cross

The Celtic Cross spread is suitable for answering a specific question. The answer describes the past, the present and issues bearing on the present, the intended objective, and the outcome. Use only the 22 major arcana cards at first, then with experience move on to use the entire deck. The reading develops in three stages:

I. Choose the card which most closely represents the questioner or the question, the Significator, and place it at the centre. The card may represent you, or the issue of the question.

The chosen Significator emphasizes one of three areas. The cards representing zodiac signs (cards 4, 5, 6, 7, 8, 9, 11, 13, 14, 15, 17, 18) indicate a process, when representing planets (1, 2, 3, 10, 16, 19, 21) show a way to behave, and when elements (1, 12, 20) show a focus upon mental, emotional or spiritual aspects of the question. For example, the Hanged Man shows feelings (the element Water) are the most important issue, the Fool shows that ideas (the element Air) are most important, and Judgement shows the energy (the element Fire) applied is most important.

In the case of a legal matter, the Justice card (Libra) would be a natural choice. For a question concerning whether or not to leave a difficult relationship, the Hanged Man (Water), the card of feelings and suspension would be an appropriate best choice. For a question whether to invest in a stock issue, the card Strength (Leo) would be appropriate as Leo governs speculation.

II. When the Significator is chosen the pack of cards is shuffled as the questioner thinks about the question, concentrating upon the Significator. The top nine cards are drawn, placed and interpreted in the following order.

The Meaning of the Celtic Cross Positions:

1. **The Significator** (the centre) – the present position of the questioner or the question.

2. **The Crossing** (on top of the Significator) – existing influences or obstacles.

3. **The Foundation** (below the Significator) – subconscious influences and the relationship of the questioner to the issue at hand.

4. **The Goal** (above the Significator) – the desired outcome of the issue.

5. **The Past** (left of the Significator) – influences in the recent or distant past which are still in operation.

6. **The Future** (right of the Significator) – influences which will come into manifestation in the near future.

The next cards are a separate file which deal with the higher issues raised in the reading.

7. **The Attitude** (bottom of the righthand row) – present position and attitude of the questioner.

8. **The Environment** (second up the row) – influences from nearby and other people.

9. **The Feelings** (third up the row) – inner hopes, fears, anxieties and secret factors not expressed about the matter.

10. **Manifestation** (top of the row) – final result and culmination of the issue.

III. The reading is interpreted by looking up the appropriate pages for each card in the reading. If the question is still unsatisfactorily answered, the tenth card, Manifestation, should be used as the Significator of a new layout. When a majority of cards are reversed, it indicates that the issue is unlikely to manifest in a positive fashion or that there are delays and obstacles in operation.

A Sample Reading using the Celtic Cross

Question: Will my business deal be successful?

1. **The Significator** – Fool (Air): chosen because the element air is mind and communication, and the Fool governs the beginning of a venture. (The major issues will be the careful consideration at the start of the venture of what is intended, a tendency to be immature but enthusiastic, and the need to be careful of naive attitudes.)

2. **The Crossing** – Moon (Pisces): obstacles from the past are preventing progress, and show hidden enemies. (Reversed, there is a danger of readily accepting existing circumstances without considering existing deception coming from outside. The questioner must be careful on the path ahead.)

3. **The Foundation** – High Priestess (Moon): wisdom and sound judgement, the potential to unite minds. The truth may be brought to consciousness through intuition and divination. (The question has an emotional foundation, and the questioner will need to act intuitively to discover the hidden truth.)

4. **The Goal** – Lovers (Gemini): a dispute arising from rigidity and the necessity to make a decision about partners. A choice with more significance than outer appearances suggest. (Cooperation is essential, and an impartial third party must be consulted.)

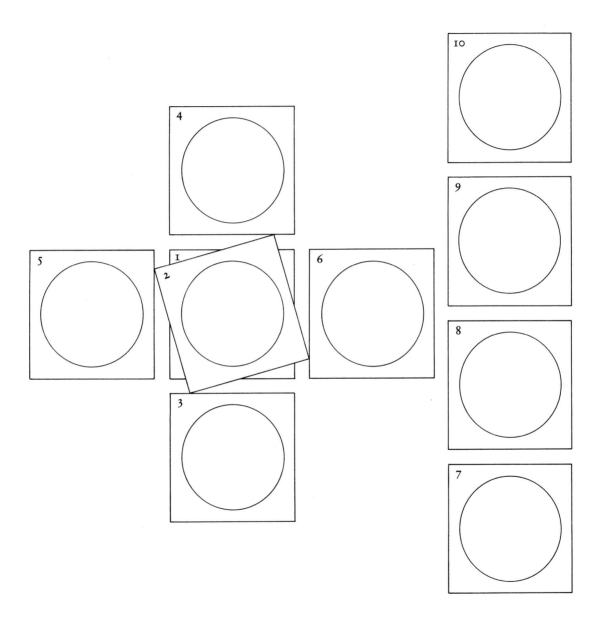

5. **The Past** – Tower (Mars): the danger of holding on to incorrect opinions, and the need for total change leading to a new beginning. (Former attitudes must be changed forcibly, and there will be an initial loss of money and personnel before a new situation is created. The blocking influence of 2 above may be eliminated.)

6. **The Future** – Magician (Mercury): active, lucid and penetrating mind gets to the bottom of a problem. (The possibility for successful change is present and flexibility is the key.)

7. **The Attitude** – Emperor (Aries): self-assertion, taking the initiative, confidence, male influence and the exercise of authority. (Reversed, the questioner is used to being totally in control, and must give up such an attitude in order to gain success.)

8. **The Environment** – Judgement (Fire and Pluto): success despite difficulties which force an about turn and the termination of current partnerships. (Leaning to the right, current associations must be terminated in order to transform the situation.)

9. **The Feelings** – High Priest (Taurus): tradition provides stability, and there is a need for generosity in ovecoming difficult attachments. (Conservative feelings lead to conviction. It is essential to create a firm structure and even to alter the physical location.)

10. **Manifestation** – Empress (Venus): the path of harmony through conflict, leading to fruitfulness and material wealth. (The result will be favourable due to strong direction, and could lead to the acquisition of property and wealth.)

Additionally, the Celtic Cross reading is a story with some general judgements which qualify the question. Reversed cards in any of the positions indicate potentially vulnerable areas which the questioner must look at very carefully. In this case the Crossing and the Attitude are reversed, showing obstacles which must be overcome by a change in attitude, while the Environment leans left, which shows the critical partnership issue that must be resolved.

The sample reading shows how the cards present many sides of a situation and embody the answers within it.

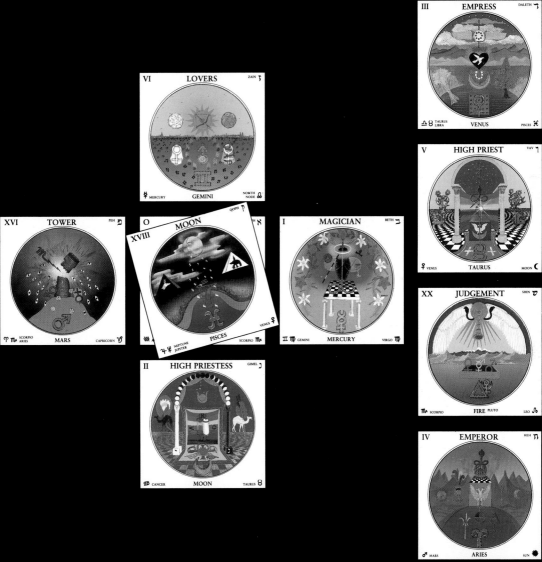

The Astrological Spread

There are many spreads which use more cards than the 10 of the Celtic Cross, including Gypsy spreads which use all the cards. For the Mandala Astrological Tarot the most important and useful complex spread is the Astrological Spread, which uses 21 cards and has the unique capacity of being applied to any period of time required by a questioner.

The basic idea of the Astrological Spread is that the sequence of 12 astrological houses is a matrix or pattern which describes any process. The spread may be used to answer a question, to provide answers when no question is formulated, and to describe a period of time.

In its structure, the Astrological Spread is an expansion of the central cross of the Celtic Cross with an astrological wheel around its periphery. The cards are placed in the following order:

1. **Significator** in the centre.

2. **Crossing** on top of the Significator.

3. **First house** of Personality. The questioner's mind, health, physical shape, appearance and personality.

4. The essence of **Personality** to the left.

5. **Second house** of the Physical World. Financial issues, losses and gains, loans, property.

6. **Third house** of Self Expression and Siblings. Brothers and sisters, short journeys, neighbours, writing, artwork, messages and messengers.

7. **Fourth house** of Home, Family, Deep Emotions. Mother, parents in general, houses and lands, towns, the end of undertakings, deep feelings, the family system.

8. The essence of **Unconsciousness**.

9. **Fifth house** of Self-consciousness and Creativity. Children, pregnancy, pleasure, gambling, speculation, teachers, education, games.

10. **Sixth house** of Work, Diet and Health. Sickness, work, daily tasks, employees, secondary school, dependants, pets.

11. **Seventh house** of Partnership and Enemies. Marriage, love affairs, description of husband or wife, contracts, partnerships, business associates, enemies, harmony and conflict.

12. The essence of **Relationship**.

13. **Eighth house** of Separation and the Metaphysical. Involvement with others, other people's emotions, ideas, possessions and energies, legacies, investments, insurance, corporations, research, death, depth psychology.

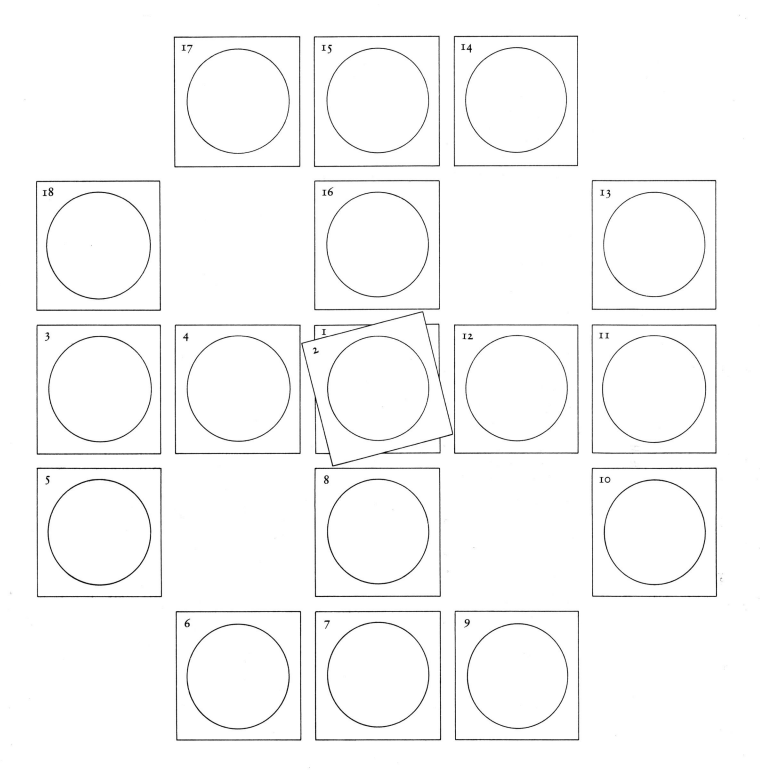

14. **Ninth house** of Higher Mind and Spiritual Aspirations. Long journeys, travel, foreign places, people and influences, expansion of consciousness, world view, religion, philosophy, psychology, books, higher education, law, publicity.

15. **Tenth house** of Conscious Aspirations and Profession. Ego-consciousness, worldly honour, wealth, standing in the community, fame, profession, judges, parents, grandfather.

16. The essence of **Ego Consciousness.**

17. **Eleventh house** of Plans, Groups and Friends. Friends and associations, hopes, desires, wishes, idealistic and altruistic interests, groupies, groups, societies, stepchildren.

18. **Twelfth house** of Psychic affairs and Secrets. Seclusion, isolation, privacy, sacrifice, outer influences beyond one's control, psychic or mystical dreams, fantasies, karmic debts, sorrow, tribulation, hidden relations, secrets, institutions, prison.

By checking the above list it is easy to determine which houses to consult for questions. Often a combination of houses will show aspects of the issue at hand.

As with all the spreads shown in the Mandala Astrological Tarot, it is possible to use either the major arcana or the entire deck.

The outer sequence of 12 house positions in the spread represent a sequence of qualities which exist through time. Consider them like the hands of a clock which may describe the time of day, or as a yearly cycle of 12 months, or as a cycle of 12 days, years or decades. Any unit of time may be made equal to each of the 12 houses.

The progression of 12 houses is the series of outer influences in operation, as indicated in the above list, and the five planets of the inner cross are the essences of the four major cardinal points of the compass. The Ascendant to the left and east is the personality. The Descendant to the right and west is relationship. The MC to the top and south is ego consciousness. The IC to the bottom and north is unconsciousness. The four cards within the cardinal power points are the essences of these qualities. Therefore, the spread has an outward Personality as the first house and a card for the essence of the Personality. The implication is that for the primary angles of the horoscope everyone has outer and inner qualities acting simultaneously, sometimes in agreement, sometimes in opposition. The cards relative to each other are very revealing.

When presenting the cards for shuffling before an Astrological Spread it is important to ask the questioner to meditate on the question and the time limit within which the question applies. Obviously, since there are 12 positions in the sequence, it is most convenient when the time period is divisible by 12, although any time period may be used and divided into 12 stages. It is appropriate to use time periods such as: 12 days (one card per day), 24 days (one card per two days), six weeks (two cards per week), 12 weeks (one card per week), six months (one card for two weeks), one year (one card per month), two years (one card per two months), etc.

Birthday readings move from the birthday at one card per month for a year. A New Year reading moves through the calendar from January to December at one card per month. Many other time periods may be used in this way.

Sample Reading using the Astrological Spread

Question: Will my boyfriend propose to me over the next year from 1 March and what direction will our relationship take?

It is important to determine which of the 12 houses will be significant for this question. The first house is the questioner's mind and personality; the fifth house is speculation, children; the seventh house is love affairs, contracts, marriage and a description of the husband; the eighth house is the financial status of the potential husband; the eleventh house is the hopes and wishes of the questioner; and the twelfth shows anything hidden about the issue.

1. **The Significator** – Chariot (Cancer): attachment to emotional bonds and the desire to create a home and family are the dominating issues. (Her feelings must be controlled and inner conflicts resolved. If she is sensitive to nurturing others, they will respond in kind.)

2. **The Crossing** – Sword Three (Uranus in Libra) leaning left: creative interests, great originality in relationships and unexpected material gain from contracts. (The questioner's own creative drive shows that her primary reason for the desired marriage is to break away from a routine with which she is bored.)

3. **First House** (month of March) – Sun (Sun): the personality of the questioner is light, self-expressive, loving and friendly. (She is friendly and her need for companionship is strong. She wants to extend her natural warmth to another person, as long as there are high ideals.)

4. **Ascendant** essence of personality – Cup Prince (Pisces): the questioner has hidden feelings of devotion. She feels destined and fated to enter this relationship. (Reversed shows that she tends to be unrealistic about herself deep inside, and can easily become emotionally dependent on others.)

5. **Second House** (month of April) – Sword Two (Venus in Libra): harmonious relationships founded on love and balance. (Reversed is scattered affections created by overidealizing her loved one. She must learn to be more realistic. The second house is the area of unreality, finances and material support.)

6. **Third House** (month of May) – Wand Two (Mars in Aries): desire for adventure which may be insensitive. (Leaning right is her boyfriend who is anxious to be independent. At this time she should not pursue him as he will only withdraw.)

7. **Fourth House** (month of June) – Cup Ten (Pluto in Pisces): artistic abilities emerge when unconscious drives have outer means for expression. (The fourth house is home and family, showing that her creative drives need the security of a committed relationship for full expression.)

8. **Essence of the IC** – Sword Eight (Mercury in Gemini): love of variety, change and originality but with little practicality. (Reversed is her quite complex emotional needs and the tension between her need for flexibility and the potential security of her desired marriage.)

9. **Fifth House** (month of July) – Wheel of Fortune (Jupiter): chance, change and the attitudes or overall view of the questioner. (A time for trying to understand what benefits can come from the possible union, amidst uncertainty and change.)

10. **Sixth House** (month of August) – Wand Five (Sun in Leo): noble and organized personality assuming command and with the authority to achieve great aspirations. (Leaning to the right is her intended partner taking command and making a proposal of marriage. The sixth house is choices and service.)

11. **Seventh House** (month of September) – Lovers (Gemini): a choice must be made between physical and emotional needs. (In the position of partnership it shows the need to consult with an impartial third party to clarify the choice and resolve inner disputes. The choice is more significant than outer appearances suggest. She has an opportunity to establish control over her own creative side.)

12. **Essence of the Partnership** – Pentacle Seven (Saturn in Taurus): a serious issue centres around material inertia and unrealistic speculation. (A conservative outlook and attention to understanding the situation is essential.)

13. **Eighth House** (month of October) – Wand Princess (Spirit): pure instinctive intellect and a superficial grasp of matters. (The questioner is leaving herself very reliant on her partner and feels it.)

14. **Ninth House** (month of November) – Wand Ace: pure energy applied to the commencement of something. Initiating activity. (A time when the relationship begins, possibly the time of marriage, and the application of all best intentions.)

15. **Tenth House** (month of December) – Cup Queen (Cancer): receptive and reflective feelings, receiving support and family acceptance. (The relationship is accepted by both families and she feels secure and supported.)

16. **Essence of the MC** – Empress (Venus): loving embrace of the world with its joys and sorrows, and contact with the deeper emotional core. (Following the path of harmony through conflict. She and the marriage are fruitful and fertile. It can indicate a deep and unexpressed wish for conception.)

17. **Eleventh House** (month of January) – Cup Princess (Emotion): grace and gentleness leading to romantic rapture and idealism. (Leaning left, she is very happy, and expresses it by making idealistic plans.)

18. **Twelfth House** (month of February) – Hermit (Virgo): transformation experienced alone. (Leaning right indicates the qualities and behaviour of her partner, which have previously been hidden, and which must be understood and overcome through thought or meditation. Withdrawal from the world is beneficial to her.)

It can be seen that the astrological reading is very specific and highly informative. If there are questions about the meaning of any of the cards in the Astrological Spread, interpretive information can be derived from standard astrological books. For example, when the card of the Moon appears in the fifth house, it could be interpreted as Pisces qualities in the fifth house, or the ruling planets Jupiter or Neptune in the fifth house.

There are many other varieties of tarot spreads which can be used and experimented with. Most gain in clarity by using the Mandala Astrological Tarot cards due to the use of astrology in addition to the traditional symbols.

Chapter 6

MEDITATION
AND
TAROT

While the obvious reason for using the tarot is divination, it is also a powerful meditation device. In meditation the emotions are made quiet and the perceptive and creative functions of the many dimensions of the mind are allowed to become manifest. Using the tarot cards as objects of meditation has the advantage of the archetypal images, colours, symbols and landscapes so vividly portrayed. Each card is an environment which looks like the outside world, but exists within the soul. Just as it is valuable to use the cards and reflect on their imagery and meanings, further meditation on them is invaluable in your quest for growth and understanding.

The mind has a great capacity to identify with, carry and process images, and once such a faculty is trained and used, it may enrich other areas of life by bringing into being wider horizons and greater openness. The focus of mental powers on particular cards is a training for concentration. Visualizing the landscapes of the major arcana also permits constant self-evaluation of the inner world and its goals, objectives and desires.

Initially it is useful to devote a short meditation session to each card, one at a time. The sequence of numbers is a good way to start. Settle yourself in a quiet room with lowered light and, if possible, direct a slightly brighter source of light on to the card.

Allow yourself to enter the landscape. Take time to see and experience all the details of the card. Notice the colours, take in their tones and variations. Sense the atmosphere of the day or night. Investigate the smells emanating from the flowers and the animals, appreciate the beauty and serenity of the scene set up for your benefit. Each card and its environment hold a key to a stage in the development of your psyche.

The landscape contains gradations of feeling, a particular atmosphere which echoes something inside you. Try to remember what it is, and notice which feelings manifest themselves in connection with details of the scene. Be aware that those parts of the card which are most vivid also represent aspects of your life and experience which are now in the process of becoming more striking and real. Allow the images to reveal their essence to you, and recognize the great value of apparently small or insignificant details of the whole.

You can enter the card and wear the crown of the king, ride the chariot of the Prince or walk the path of the Hermit to enlightenment. Step into the scene, adopt the ritual poses indicated and imagine yourself donning the identity of the figures. Each card is a stage of initiation, and as you identify with it, feel what it is like, be permeated by the energies of the card, and see how you can become the Emperor or the Moon. The images can either provide you with identity, or free you from qualities which entrap you. The choice is yours.

Other related images may arise in the course of meditating upon a card. Just let the images come, make them more real, smell them, touch them and absorb them. Take in and experience their qualities fully. Consider what they mean to you and how they might affect your life.

Meditation upon the tarot images is a two-fold operation. One aspect of such meditation leads to an intimate feeling about, and understanding of, the cards as a sequence of stages in the discovery of the world and the Self. The second stage is to bring the desired qualities represented by the cards into the reality of your life and relationships. Each card is a cypher or symbol of a particular way of being, and either you already enact the principles and wish to strengthen them or use them more effectively, or you feel you lack them and wish to bring them into your being. Either way, the use of, and meditation upon, the Mandala Astrological Tarot is a step on the path to enlightenment.